ERIC WAREHEIM

WITH **EMILY TIMBERLAKE**

FOODHEIM

A CULINARY ADVENTURE

10
TEN SPEED PRESS
California | New York

PHOTOGRAPHS BY JULIA STOTZ
ART BY DUKE ABER
CREATIVE CONSULTING BY MADISON BORBELY

Contents

To my mommer, Edeltraud Wareheim.

Introduction

HI! I'M ERIC.

SOME PEOPLE CALL ME HEIMY.

I'M 6 FEET, 7 INCHES TALL

AND I LOVE SPOOFS & GOOFS,

FOOD, WINE & CATS.

The HeimLine

My first hero was C.C. DeVille, the guitarist from Poison. He introduced me to the whammy bar. When I was fourteen, I was on the JV basketball team and was awarded a printed certificate for being the first-ever student in my high school to slam dunk. To this day, I still respect the art of a heavy-metal guitar solo as well as the graceful power of a slam dunk.

I have the same reverence and respect when it comes to food and wine. I remember the first time that I encountered shrimp cocktail with a spicy horseradish dipper. I was overcome with emotion, just like the first time I listened to "Talk Dirty to Me." These are the moments that shaped Heimy.

I don't just love food and wine. I worship it. I study it. It's been this way ever since I was a little kid.

I was born in Baltimore. When I was just a tot, my family would take trips to nearby Ocean City. I credit those early vacations with my passion for blue crab, Old Bay Seasoning, summer produce, and, of course, boardwalk fries! Those extra-crispy fries doused with malt vinegar were one of my first food crushes.

When we moved to Audubon, Pennsylvania, I led a normal food-boy life, eating the stuff that most kids in the suburbs ate in those days. But I was lucky because my mom had a vegetable garden and baked her own bread. My friends and I obsessed over it. When I wasn't misbehaving, my mom would give me a piece of warm bread with a smear of Brie and I'd go psycho. In those days I was a Boy Scout, and, one year, I won the Box Car Derby with my dad's help (he hid melted fishing weights inside the wood car frame). We celebrated afterward with Pizza Hut personal pan pies, all buttery, salty deliciousness. I loved that it was just for me—no sharing with my sister, Jessica!

My maternal grandparents lived in Germany, and the few trips we took to visit them solidified my love for German village cuisine: schnitzels, stews, rouladen. Oma and Opa were so frugal. They'd take cheap cuts of meat and simmer them for hours to create a cauldron of happiness and flavor. I'd watch Opa go to the garden to clip herbs for his world-famous Opa Salad (page 206). Then he'd come in and ask my sister and me why we drank straight orange soda. It was horrifying for him to see his blood relatives not cut that sugary syrup with some sparkling water.

I moved to Philadelphia for college, and for the next five years I was vegetarian. It was pretty much a nightmare. Whole Foods did not exist. A dry veggie patty on a previously frozen bagel was a highlight in those days. When I started eating meat again, I branched out a bit more but really focused on my favorites: pizza, cheesesteaks, and Italian American cuisine.

Immediately after college I got a job as an assistant wedding videographer. I wore a fake silk blouse with one large, gold top button. My boss taught me how to back up to the shrimp table and sneak a bite while pretending to take pictures. As a photographer, you were allowed only a crappy cold sandwich, but I usually left these events full of premium sea meats due to my shrimp theft skills. I got to the point where I could grab a shrimp, dip it in some cocktail sauce, and pop it in my mouth while simultaneously posing the bride and her bridesmaids.

It wasn't until I moved to Los Angeles and started exploring all the global goodness that the city had to offer that my love for food really went to the next level. Mexican food, Thai food, sushi, farmers' markets; you name it, things were popping! I started traveling around the world—to Mexico, Japan, Thailand, Italy, France, and more—and my interest in regional food traditions kept growing. Then I started touring with my comedy partner, Tim Heidecker.

I attribute my great awakening to the art and beauty of food to one meal: at Alinea, in Chicago. Tim and I were touring and I had a day off. Somehow I got a res at this three-Michelin-starred food mecca, which is considered one of the top restaurants in the world. Alinea has a dress code but I didn't have a blazer, so I asked my hotel if they had anything I could borrow. I was in luck! They had Michael Jordan's jacket from a photo shoot many years prior. They offered it to me if I promised to return it. MICHAEL JORDAN'S BLAZER!!! WHAT?! I put it on. It was way too big, but it gave me superpowers. I rolled into Alinea like I owned the place, then proceeded to have the most magical, entertaining meal. I was blown away by the artistry, including chef Dave Beran himself plating the "entire table" dessert in front of me. Wow.

From Food Boy to Food Man

Today, I run a number-one-rated, award-winning Top Food Blog and spend most of my time as a pasta photographer. I often wear matching Tevas with my Madi, and sometimes carry my cat around in a BabyBjörn. Nothing makes me happier than

cooking gorgeous meals at home. Sometimes it's a twenty-minute pasta al pomodoro with perfectly ripe, perfectly in-season farmers' market tomatoes. Sometimes it's an elaborate, weekend-warrior-style project, like pizza dough from scratch or a dankadent array of raw-fish dishes. My life has come full circle because now I know how to bake that Pizza Hut–style personal pan pizza at home (see page 86). And I wanna teach you all my tricks.

My food obsession may seem surprising to people who know me for my comedy work. But I've been into culinary delights for at least as long as I've been into professional comedy—they're both essential parts of the Complete Heimy Experience. And to me, there's always been a connection between the two. More specifically, a connection between chefs and comedy people: We're all freaks.

The food industry and comedy biz are both known for attracting outsiders—intense, talented weirdos who don't really fit in to mainstream society. That's why I've always felt a bond with chefs. We're all obsessive, over-the-top people. Our parents worry about our life choices. We're super-focused on our craft and take our work very seriously—but we also live life to the fullest and like to have a good time. That's why so many comedy people are also food people. If you're traveling to a new town and want to know the best spot for lunch, a late-night meal, or a cool quiet bar, ask a comedy person who tours a lot—they always have the best tips.

Back in 2009, me and my comedy friends Aziz Ansari, Alan Yang, and Jason Woliner started something we called "Food Club." Basically, we showed up to fancy restaurants wearing suits and captains' hats. If we liked the meal, we awarded the chef with a plaque. If we didn't like the meal, we burned the plaque in front of the restaurant. A few of the plaques are still hanging in restaurants in LA, and a pilot we shot for a *Food Club* TV show is online somewhere.

Food Club started as a total joke—a way for us to kind of poke fun at fine-dining culture and its old-school, rich-guy stuffiness. But it also exposed us to so much greatness. We were moved by the quality and creativity of the food. And in some cases, we got to befriend the chefs. Jon Shook and Vinny Dotolo, two of the greatest chefs in the modern LA food scene, became official skippers. We presented them with tiny skipper hats and they took us around the city to all their spots—incredible restaurants, like Totoraku—and started to turn us on to the real-deal food and wine scene.

In a lot of ways, comedy is what allowed me to live out my wildest food fantasies. While Tim & Eric was touring, I got to meet barbecue-god Aaron Franklin in Austin, where he fed me meltingly tender bites of brisket that he'd smoked in an old oil drum for sixteen hours. After one of my live shows in London, I slammed gin martinis with Anthony Bourdain at Groucho's in Soho. (Miss you, man.) When I was filming *Master of None,* I relocated to NYC, and Aziz and I would choose shooting locations based on their proximity to yummy spots where we wanted to eat after wrapping. That's how we ended up shooting at pasta paradise il Buco, The Four Horsemen, and Mission. This is a very annoying and braggy way of saying, *Thank you, Comedy Gods, for allowing all of this to happen.*

In between projects, I always try to fly somewhere new to immerse myself in the food culture. That could be anywhere from San Sebástian in the Spanish Basque Country, where I went on bonk "pintxos crawls" and hopped from bar to bar snacking on tinned fish and croquetas, to Japan, where sushi masters prepared omakase experiences that were so mind-blowingly beautiful and perfect, they literally made me cry. Thank you, Sawada San.

That's what inspired me to write this book—my desire to share all the incredible things I've learned by traveling the world these last fifteen years in search of the most premium bites. Because at the end of the day, cooking is about bringing people together, taking the time to prepare something special, and sharing it with someone you care about. This is the book I wish I had when I first started messing around in the kitchen.

As I started thinking about and developing recipes for all of my favorite things to eat—dishes I consider the "Heimy classics" that everyone should try—I realized that there's a really wide range, from elegant sashimi preparations to a simple pepperoni pizza. I think that balance is important for a well-rounded food connoisseur. On the one hand, I'm sometimes a fancy boy who enjoys wagyu rib-eyes and premium red Carabinero prawns flown in from Spain. On the other hand, I get emotional and teary-eyed when I think about homey, German village food, like the schnitzel that my mom used to make for me. I wouldn't be Chef Heimy if it weren't for Oma and Opa in Germany, who taught me that nothing in the world tastes better than tomatoes picked straight from your garden, still slightly warm from the sun, and that I should not be a wasteful American and should shut up and appreciate what my elders are saying to me.

I've dined at nustso spots, like Noma, but I haven't forgotten my roots. In college, my food budget was three dollars per day, which would buy me a tofu bánh mì from the local Vietnamese sandwich shop and an Olde English forty from the bodega. When I got to LA and had a few bucks, I was finally able to check out elegant, tasting-menu spots. The funny thing is, now I mostly prefer simple, ingredient-driven cooking rather than elaborate technique and three Michelin stars. I'm back on hoagies, and one of my favorite meals in LA is the Padrino sandwich from Pizzana. It delivers a feeling of home, happiness, and comfort. As it turns out, that's all I'm looking for these days.

All the recipes you'll find here honor a stage of my culinary journey. This book is all of my favorite things. It's from my heart and I made it especially for YOU. You'll find recipes inspired by bites I've tasted on the road—for example, a panzanella with the freshest summer veg I had on vacation in Rome (see page 210), or a fried grouper sandwich from an amazing fish shack on the Gulf Coast of Florida (see page 31). But there are also a lot of callbacks to the food of my childhood. Simple, comforting dishes that my mom or my oma and opa used to make. Lots of sandwiches, because one of my first jobs was at Subway, where I had a crush on my goth manager who taught me the art of the sandwich. (We called her Raven and she blasted Siouxsie and the Banshees on the radio. She would compliment me on my mopping skills and I would get goose bumps.) Elevated versions of classics, like pan pizza (see page 86) and orange chicken (see page 154), that I loved as a kid in the suburbs. An addictive nonna sauce (see page 109) so powerful in flavor that you will never want to visit a Buca di Beppo ever again.

My biggest goals with this book are to help people who aren't super-confident in the kitchen and prove to them that cooking doesn't have to be this complicated, intimidating thing. I'm not a chef; I didn't go to culinary school. I'm just someone who gets passionate about things—art, music, comedy, food—and eventually tries to figure out how to do it myself. Your first attempts might not be amazing; but if you keep practicing and experimenting, eventually you'll come up with something you love and have that incredible "I MADE THIS!" moment.

All you really need is to start with good ingredients and treat them with respect. So, invest in nice, in-season farmers' market produce, high-quality olive oil and cheeses, and organic meat and fish. From there, play around with flavors and combinations that speak to you. Experiment, with the ultimate goal of elevating (rather than concealing) the true flavors of your ingredients. Invite some friends, pour some good wines, and imagine my voice whispering in your ear, giving you li'l pep talks as you embark on this culinary journey.

MISTER
DIPPER

ERIC'S CULINARY GLOSSARY

Here are some official food terms you'll see throughout the book.

acid freak (noun)

1 Someone who subscribes to my food and wine philosophy: ACID IS ESSENTIAL! Say no to flabby wines and unbalanced foods. Everything tastes better with the electric zing of acid, whether it's from freshly squeezed citrus or a nice vinegar.

bonk (adjective)

1 Short for *bonkers*

2 A wildly amazing taste or dish or experience

Chef's Kiss (noun)

1 When you nail a dish and blow it a kiss as a sign of respect

2 A secret language among chefs used to praise one another

dankadence (noun)

1 Deep, robust flavors

2 The most outrageously delicious wines, soulful bites, and mind-blowing culinary experiences

3 The highest plane of existence on the Heimy Happiness Hierarchy (HHH)

gorg (adjective)

1 Short for *gorgeous*

2 A dish that uses the freshest, in-season produce and highest-quality pantry ingredients

3 A dish that ENERGIZES you as you eat it rather than putting you in a food coma

Heimy-style, #HeimyStyle (adjective)

1 Food presented in a perfectly circular manner (e.g., shrimp fanned in an attractive pinwheel, white bread cut into circles for a sandwich, or fried eggs cooked in a ring mold)

2 Food finished with beautiful, flaky sea salt (such as Maldon) and a generous drizzle of extra-virgin olive oil

3 Rich, fatty food balanced with tons of fresh herbs and a splash of acid

oh mama! (interjection)

1 Highest possible praise for a dish, especially a dish that is Italian American in origin

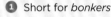

HEIMY HAPPINESS HIERARCHY (HHH)

About This Book

I've divided this book into nine chapters, each covering a different element of the Complete Heimy Experience. First up is Circle Foods, which are an essential part of my diet. I'm talking burgers, tacos, tostadas. Any member of the larger family of circular sandwiches. There's a reason so many ancient religions worshipped circles; it's a perfect shape. There's no start or end, there is just CIRCLE. Full bliss and enlightenment. For me, circle foods are utensils-free; I like to eat them with my hands, so there's no fork or knife standing between me and divine, circular deliciousness.

The king of all circle foods is, of course, the Pizza, so I devote an entire chapter to this holy food. I share everything I've learned from meticulous on-the-ground research and the hundreds of pies I've made in my home kitchen as well as tasted around the world.

The next chapter is devoted to what I like to call Grandma Foods. My oma and opa in Germany were the ones who taught me about the beauty of simple, unpretentious village food: salads picked fresh from the kitchen garden, potatoes with butter and chives, low and slow braises. To cook well, you don't need to spend a ton of money; Grandma Food is about making the most of a few impeccably sourced ingredients. The best pasta you've ever had in your life requires only eggs, flour, water, and patience. Take the time to talk to your dough. Tell it you love it. Tell it you're proud of its gluten development. Thank it. Tell it that it's about to find a beautiful new home alongside your homemade tomato sauce.

There's the Chicken Chapter, because I CHERISH CHICKEN! You want my fried chicken recipe? Well, how about two fried chicken recipes? How about three? HOW ABOUT FOUR GOD-DAMN FRIED CHICKEN RECIPES?! Heimy's got you. Pretty much every global food culture has its own version, so I've included some of my personal favorites to make at home. Chicken done right will blow your mind. While we're talking chicky, I have to share my Golden Chicken Rule: Always buy organic, humanely raised birds. (This goes for all meat, in fact.) I care about the planet. I care about you. And I care about the quality of what is going in your body. There is no sense putting in all this work if your meat is subpar. A low-stress bird that has room to roam during its life will make a dramatically more flavorful experience. Once you have this protein aha moment, you'll start to hold back on the extra seasonings to let the natural flavors shine through. It's a beautiful thing. So, find a good butcher or two who sells sustainable meat. Make friends with them. They are the gatekeepers to deliciousness.

Juicy Foods are gorgeous, showstopping main dishes to impress your close friends and fam. I'm gonna teach you top-secret techniques to perfectly grill intimidating, big, bone-in steaks to medium-rare and make fall-off-the-bone tender pork ribs with a magical sauce.

If you really want to experience the Heimy Lifestyle and not burn out in five years, you must incorporate glorious Green Foods. I devoted this chapter to crisp salads and other vegetable-centric dishes that will move you. Green is gorgeous and can be wildly flavorful when prepared with some love. I was vegetarian for five years in my early twenties. It was a nightmare of grilled cheeses and boring prepackaged salads. But things are different now and Green is Good!

The last two chapters of this book are devoted to Wine-Heim and Cocktails. One of the great privileges of my life has been to meet and befriend so many amazing winemakers, importers, and sommeliers, who have shared their wines and expertise with me. My goal is to return the favor by demystifying the world of wine, sharing tips for finding delicious, conscientiously made, low-intervention wines wherever you are. The world of wine and spirits may seem intimidating at first, but it really doesn't have to be. All you need is an open mind.

But all these chapters mean nothing if you don't follow the most important tenet of my life's philosophy, that you must share your riches with your friends. Giving the gift of food is truly one of the most meaningful gestures. Go all out. Make it unforgettable. Prepare some of these recipes, invite over your closest friends, and make it a memorable night. What's more significant than food 'n' friends, really? So, throughout this book, I'll share several party play-by-plays, with tips on food and wine pairings, pre-party prep, and menu ideas. Good food, good drinks, good friends—these are the keys to a good life.

GOOD FOOD   GOOD DRINKS   GOOD FRIENDS

Eric's Essentials

Ideally, this book will push you out of your comfort zone a bit, encouraging you to discover new ingredients and dishes and inspiring you to amp up the quality of the ingredients you buy regularly—oils, vinegars, anchovies. These simple ingredients can totally elevate your cooking and will give you a newfound respect for classic dishes. (Good Parmigiano means good pasta!)

Here's a Heimy hot-tip to help you stock your pantry: If you eat something amazing at a restaurant, ask why it's so amazing. I developed my ceviche recipe (see page 182) by being very annoying at my local Peruvian spot. They gave me tips on where to buy the cancha, and they actually sold me the aji peppers!

I really hope this book will inspire you to talk to people at your favorite restaurants, to learn more about their cuisine. Don't just be a food tourist. At the very least, do some Googling to find regional specialty shops, like an Italian market to buy the best imported Calabrian chile and balsamic vinegar; a Japanese market to buy shoyu, premium short-grain rice, and nori; a Thai market to buy Thai eggplants, curry paste, and makrut lime leaves. These ingredients will be so much better than what you find at chain grocery stores, even "fancy" chain grocery stores.

Ingredients

If you want to truly get in the Heimy Mindset, your pantry will always have the following ingredients.

Anchovies: I'm a fish freak and so I always have tons of tinned fish (see "My Favorite Fishies," page 219) in my pantry. Anchovies are a special favorite. I love Ortiz, a Spanish brand that comes in jars or tins. They are pricey compared to the crappy options but invest in that flavor!

Capers and **caperberries:** These are some of my all-time favorite and most-used ingredients. You can buy capers either in brine or packed in salt. Soak salt-packed capers in water for 20 minutes before using—the flavor is worth the wait. Caperberries are the big-boy version of the tiny caper buds you are used to seeing at your bagel shop. They're amazing on a pizza (see page 77).

Cheese: Specifically, you've gotta have Parmigiano-Reggiano and Pecorino Romano on hand at *all* times. Buy the nicest stuff you can afford. Don't you DARE look at the pre-shredded or pre-grated stuff. Get big hunks from a cheesemonger and take the time to grate it fresh every time you cook. It takes 30 seconds and makes all the difference. Save the rinds in your fridge to add a savory note to soups and stews.

For pizza, buy firm, whole-milk mozzarella (it is often labeled as "low-moisture")—this is *not* the kind that comes in brine (only my CheeseHeim on page 73 uses fior di latte); it is usually sold as a log and vacuum-sealed. Again, step away from the pre-shredded stuff, which has all sorts of weird preservatives.

Garlic and **shallots:** Never leave the grocery store without them. Buy whole heads of garlic rather than the pre-peeled cloves. If you see a little green guy popping out of the top of a garlic clove, take the time to remove the sprout with your knife. (This sprout is called the "germ" and tends to be unpleasantly bitter.)

Herbs and **spices:** Wherever possible, I like to buy whole spices, like cumin seed and white and black peppercorns, and grind them by hand (see "Heimy's Hint," at left). Whole spices stay fresher longer than ground spices, which lose their punchiness really quickly. I buy dried whole branches of Sicilian oregano from an Italian specialty food store. Just shake the branch over whatever food you want to season and the little dried leaves will come falling down, like snow falling from the sky. Store the whole branches in a ziplock bag in the pantry.

Heimy's Hint

If you don't have a mortar and pestle (and even if you do—I often find crushing spherical spices, like peppercorns and coriander, a pain when I do it in the mortar, because they fly everywhere), here's an easy way to crush whole spices. Place the peppercorns (or whatever spice you're using) on a cutting board. Using a clean pot or skillet, crush the peppercorns by pressing the bottom of the pot into the seeds, slowly moving the pot back and forth until the peppercorns are broken into coarse powder with a few bigger pieces.

Olive oil: You're going to need at least two olive oils in your pantry (I like Bariani and Nuñez de Prado). Always buy extra-virgin olive oil—first, a good-quality workhorse olive oil that you can use for sautéing. It doesn't have to be crazy expensive, but it should taste good. Then, you're going to need a quality finishing oil—go for the nicest stuff you can afford. And drizzle it liberally over *everything*—pizzas, pastas, salads, steaks. Sometimes I just pour it on a plate, season it with salt, and dip bread in it for the best and easiest snack. Do me a favor and toss out the bottle that has been open in the back of your pantry for three years. It's probably gone rancid.

Olives: Don't buy pitted olives; they're never as good as whole olives. Go for the varieties that look freshest and take the time to pit them yourself.

Red pepper flakes: I'm a spicy boy, which means I love to liven things up with fiery dried red pepper flakes. My favorite brand is Tuttocalabria, which sells dried crushed Calabrian chile from Southern Italy. (Try their Peperoncino in Pezzi.) You can buy the brand online or at Italian specialty stores.

Salts: You'll need kosher salt for cooking (Diamond is my preferred brand) and a flaky sea salt for finishing (I like Maldon).

Vinegars: One of my spiritual homes is Emilia-Romagna, the region in Italy where we filmed the second season of *Master of None.* Emilia-Romagna happens to be the birthplace of balsamic vinegar, so you won't be surprised to hear I take balsamic *very* seriously. When we were filming, one of our Modena friends gave me a bottle of her personal balsamic vinegar. When I say "her personal vinegar," I mean it. It's a tradition there to have a batch of balsamic started the day you're born, so this was a 30-year-old balsamic. I cherish it so much. You don't have to get *that* fancy, but look for an aged

Italian balsamic that is thick and syrupy. In addition to that, you should stock more everyday vinegars, like apple cider vinegar, rice wine vinegar, and red wine vinegar. Not all vinegars are alike. I recently stumbled onto the O-Med brand of Spanish vinegars that changed up my cooking game entirely. A lot of their vinegars have a natural sweetness, so I stopped adding sugar or honey to my dressings altogether.

Whole canned tomatoes: Always buy *whole* canned tomatoes rather than crushed tomatoes. Tomato manufacturers save their best product for the "whole" cans and sell the second-tier stuff as "crushed" or "puree." You will hear me talk a lot about San Marzano tomatoes from Southern Italy. The best ones are grown in the shadow of Mount Vesuvius, and they will truly blow your mind. BUT! There are a lot of imposters out there. So, when you're shopping for canned tomatoes, look for the DOP label. *DOP* stands for *denominazione di origine protetta*—that means you're getting the real deal, as opposed to domestic American tomatoes that are just pretending to be San Marzano. That said, there is one domestic tomato brand that I love and use all the time—my friend Chris Bianco has a line of organic canned tomatoes called Bianco DiNapoli. They're grown in Yolo County, California, and they are incredible—a totally worthy substitution for DOP Italian tomatoes.

Equipment

The right tools really make all the difference when you're cooking Heimy-style. Add these essentials to your holiday or birthday wishlist; I promise you'll thank me!

Candy thermometer: For our purposes, this will also be known as a deep-fry thermometer. This clips onto the side of your pot and helps you measure the temperature of your frying oil. You're going to be frying *a lot!*

Ceramic plateware: Toss the Ikea stuff, ask your parents for a set of their vintage stuff, or splurge on a set from a cool ceramicist, like Heath. As a hypervisual person, I find it just adds so much to see all your hard work presented in something beautiful.

Cocktail glassware: Get nice, all-purpose coupe glasses, rocks glasses for amaro, and Collins or highball glasses.

Dough scraper: This plastic tool costs just a few dollars and will make pizza dough shaping way easier and less sticky. You can also use it for transferring prepped ingredients from your cutting board to your bowl.

Dutch oven or **heavy-bottomed saucepan:** You want to deep-fry in a tall pot with high-enough sides so the oil doesn't splatter everywhere. A heavy bottom is important to conduct the heat more evenly, and to prevent hot spots that scorch the bottom of the pot.

Instant-read thermometer: You need this for making sure your steaks and chickens are cooked perfectly.

Kitchen scale: The pizza dough recipes in this book list ingredients by weight (grams) and volume (cups, tablespoons, teaspoons). If I can convince you to buy one special gadget for your kitchen, let it be a kitchen scale. Measuring ingredients by weight is so much easier than taking out all your measuring cups and spoons and getting them all dirty and then having a sink full of measuring implements to clean. Measuring by weight is also more accurate than measuring by volume. Accuracy is important here, because dough recipes can be kind of finicky. Your 1 cup of flour might be different than my 1 cup of flour if you pack the flour down, or heap it over the edge of the measuring cup, or do something weird to it that I can't even imagine. No matter what, 100 grams of flour is 100 grams of flour.

Knives: Invest in a high-quality chef's knife and keep it sharp. This means you should carefully wash and dry it by hand and store it somewhere safe. In addition to my chef's knife, I have a smaller paring knife and a serrated knife for bread. That's really all you need.

Microplane grater: This is great for many things—cheese, citrus zest, ginger, garlic.

Pans: If you buy only one, make it a 12-inch stainless-steel frying pan. My preferred brand is Made In. If you want to get fancy, buy a cast-iron skillet too. Never wash cast iron with soap; just use warm water and some elbow grease.

Pizza peels: You're definitely going to need at least one pizza peel to transfer your pizzas onto the pizza stone. I actually have two pizza peels, because I like to dress the pie on a wooden peel, which is best for transferring the pie to the stone. Then I use a metal peel to rotate the pizza and pull it from the oven, because the narrower lip of the peel makes it easier to move the pie.

Pizza stone or **steel:** This is a MUST. With pizza, the trick is to get the crust to caramelize without it drying out too much. If too much water evaporates during cooking, you're going to end up with a dry, brittle crust. A traditional wood-fired pizza oven gets up to somewhere around 900°F. Your home oven isn't getting anywhere close to that, so a pizza stone helps bridge the gap. It conducts heat, so when you lay your raw dough on it, the pizza's bottom chars and blisters really fast. Make sure to keep it clean—no excess flour, which can burn and result in charred raw-flour bites.

Plastic dough bins/tubs: These aren't essential, but they're helpful. If you want to step up your pizza game, buy a dough tub or two—you can find them at kitchen supply stores. You can use a deeper tub to mix dough in; I have a 12 by 10 by 5½-inch plastic tub with a lid that is great for storing airtight in the fridge. Then, I have a shallower, rectangular tub that's about 12 by 20 by 4 inches with a lid, which is perfect for storing your dough-ball cuties while they rise.

Rice cooker: Never cook sad, squishy rice again! This electric appliance takes out all the guesswork, and many models sing a happy li'l tune as they're working.

Wine glasses: Say nish to stemless glasses—stems are there for a reason.

HI, DOUGH BABIES!

A circle is a symbol of harmony.

It's a perfect shape, with no beginning and no end. It's a metaphor for my culinary journey. I pray to thee, goddess of circular treats and treasures. And when my earthly body retires, I shall be memorialized with a circle-shaped sarcophagus and placed right next to the Rocky statue in Philadelphia. Just make my tomb a little smaller, to respect my Balboa. The most important things the recipes in this chapter have in common is that they're all CIRCLES and delicious. They are inspired by some of my favorite circular food memories: eating sushi in Japan, or judging the ratio of blue crab to filler in crab cakes with my grandma in Maryland. (She would NEVER eat a crab cake outside of Maryland. NEVER.) Hopefully cooking these dishes will get you in a circular state of mind. They will make you question many things about food and life itself. You'll start looking at all of your favorite foods and ask yourself, "Can I make this into a circle?" The answer is almost always yes. Now you are a Circle Freak just like me.

SMASHHEIM

MAKES 4 BURGERS

I used to be a BIG burger guy—huge thick patty, big bread bun, dozens of toppings layered five feet high. The type of burger that takes major squeezing to fit in your mouth and then 50 percent of the burger slips out onto your white blouse. Damn it!

A SmashHeim, though, has the perfect size and proportions. It's a tasty little beef treat but with huge flavor and juiciness, like the griddled burgers of your fave childhood fast-food spots, but WAY better. Treat each component properly and you will be rewarded with a mind-blowing burger experience.

The process is simple: Grab a little fistful of ground beef mixed with bacon. The bacon adds a deep smoky flavor and salt component that is next level. Roll the beef-bacon mixture into a ball between your palms. Get your cast-iron skillet screaming-hot, then throw that ball into the pan and smash it down—a metal spatula is your friend. After a quick minute, flip and top with cheese.

Keep in mind that these are on the smaller side, so if you're a "Triple B" (Big Beef Boy), you might want to plan on two burgers per person.

1 In a large bowl, combine the beef and bacon and mix together with your hands. Form the meat into four equal-size balls and season liberally with salt and pepper. Set aside.

2 If you're cooking outdoors, heat your grill as hot as it will go—575°F is the target temperature. If you're cooking inside, open some windows and turn on your stove fan—things are going to get smoky.

3 Place a large cast-iron skillet or griddle on the grill or over high heat on your stove top. While it's heating up, generously coat the cut sides of each hamburger bun with some butter, then, working in batches, place the hamburger buns, buttered-side down, into the pan and toast until golden, about 1 minute. Set aside until it's time to assemble the burgies.

4 Grab one of your beef balls and a 6-inch-square piece of parchment paper. Place a generous pat of butter (about 1 tablespoon) in the preheated skillet, then place the ball on top of the butter and cover it with the parchment. (I put on an oven mitt at this point because the hot grease is gonna do some spittin'!) Using a metal spatula, a smaller skillet, or any other flat heavy surface, smash the burger as thin as it'll go to ensure that crisp char. Peel off the parchment, then cook the burger until the bottom is super-duper crispy, about 90 seconds.

10 ounces ground beef (at least 20% fat)

2 ounces bacon, chopped (about ¼ cup)

Kosher salt and freshly ground black pepper

4 Martin's potato rolls or other hamburger buns

Unsalted butter for the buns, plus ¼ cup, at room temperature

4 slices American cheese

Dill pickles for topping

¼ cup diced white onion

¼ cup Heimy's Secret Sauce (recipe follows)

continued

⑤ Flip the burger and top with a slice of cheese. Close the lid of the grill (or, if you're cooking indoors, cover the skillet with a lid or plate), just until the cheese is melted, about 30 seconds. The burger will be nicely charred on the outside.

⑥ Place the patty on a bottom bun, then top with some dill pickles and a fourth of the diced onion. Slather a generous smear of secret sauce on the top bun and close the burger. Repeat this process with the remaining balls of beef. Your SmashHeims are complete.

HEIMY'S SECRET SAUCE

MAKES ABOUT ¾ CUP

¼ cup ketchup

¼ cup mayonnaise

¼ cup yellow mustard

1 tablespoon dill relish

½ teaspoon mustard powder

In a medium bowl, combine all the ingredients and whisk until incorporated. Store airtight in the fridge for up to 1 week.

PORK DORK

MAKES 4 SERVINGS

I love circles. I need circles. I crave circles.

This Pork Dork is inspired by the tonkatsu sandwiches I'd snack on at every opportunity while traveling through Japan. At convenience stores and even on the fancy high-speed trains, you can order one of these perfect li'l prepackaged sando gems and they taste AMAZING. For me, it's all about the interplay of the two textures: crispy pork and soft bread—and the contrast of the sweet katsu sauce with the spicy mustard.

That super-soft, sweet, pillowy white bread is key here. In Japan, they use milk bread, which is harder to find in the United States. (Bub and Grandma's Bread in Los Angeles makes a great version of this stuff.) Next best would be to use brioche. White sandwich bread is an okay option as well. I like a li'l color on the top piece of bread. If you are a purist and like it spongy, you can skip the toasting step.

The one issue I have with these Japanese sandos is that they are traditionally served in squares, so I had to go Heimy-style on them and cut everything into perfect circles. Deal with it!

8 slices milk bread, brioche, or white Wonder bread, cut into perfect circles

One 3-inch-thick piece boneless pork loin (12 to 15 ounces), excess fat trimmed

Kosher salt and freshly ground black pepper

1 cup all-purpose flour

2 eggs

1 teaspoon Japanese hot mustard, plus more for serving

2 cups panko bread crumbs, or as needed

Peanut oil for frying

Katsu Sauce (recipe follows) for serving

½ head green cabbage, cored and shaved as thinly as possible

① Preheat your oven's broiler. Place the bread slices on a baking sheet and place on the middle rack of the oven. Watching VERY closely, toast the bread just until the top is golden, 30 to 60 seconds. Set aside.

② Cut the pork loin into four equal-size medallions. Place a layer of parchment paper or plastic wrap on your work surface, then place a piece of pork on top and cover with another layer of parchment or plastic. Using a kitchen mallet or a rolling pin, pound the pork a few times until it's ½ inch thick. (I like to go the extra mile and, using a paring knife, trim the medallion into a perfect circle, using a ring mold as a guide.) Repeat with the remaining pieces of pork. Season each with salt and pepper.

③ Fill a large bowl with the flour, then stir in 3 teaspoons salt. In a separate bowl, crack the eggs, add the hot mustard, and beat lightly with a fork. Place the panko in a third large bowl.

④ Working with one piece of pork at a time, dip both sides into the flour, then shake off the excess. Dip into the eggs and allow any excess to drip off. Then dip into the panko to coat both sides, pressing to make sure the panko really coats the surface of the pork. (Refresh the panko as needed.)

⑤ Fill a flat, heavy-bottomed frying pan with enough peanut oil to come halfway up the sides of the pork and set over medium-high heat. The target temperature is 345°F on a deep-frying thermometer, or you can drop a bit of panko into the pan to test whether the oil is hot enough (it should sizzle).

continued

PORK DORK,
CONTINUED

6 Depending on the size of your pan, you can fry one or two pork pieces at a time, making sure not to overcrowd the pan. Place the pork into the oil and fry until deep golden brown, 4 to 5 minutes, flipping halfway through. Transfer to a wire rack to drain as you cook the remaining pork.

7 Smear some hot mustard onto a piece of the bread; top with a piece of pork, a spoonful of katsu sauce, and a generous handful of shredded cabbage; and then top with another bread circle. Repeat with the remaining ingredients and serve immediately.

KATSU SAUCE

MAKES ABOUT ½ CUP

⅓ cup ketchup

1 tablespoon
Worcestershire sauce

1 tablespoon soy sauce

1 teaspoon packed
brown sugar

1 teaspoon kosher salt

½ teaspoon grated garlic

½ teaspoon grated ginger

In a small bowl, combine all the ingredients and whisk until incorporated. Store airtight in the fridge for up to 1 week.

JAPAN: DON'T FIT,
DON'T CARE

FISH FREAK
WITH FANCY SAUCE

MAKES 4 SERVINGS

The Gulf of Mexico holds a special place in my heart. I spent a lot of time in Apalachicola, on the Florida panhandle, with my friends from Philadelphia when I was in my twenties. Apalach has amazing white-sand beaches and it's a damn seafood paradise! We'd head down to the docks and buy a bushel of oysters—that's about sixty pounds—from the oystermen, to shuck over the course of the next few days. Inevitably we'd tear through them in two days, when we'd head back to the dock and re-up with another bushel and bags of fresh-caught shrimp.

That's where I was first introduced to the glory of the Gulf-style fried-fish sandwich. Down there, it's often made with grouper, line-caught that day and deep-fried to golden perfection.

Years later, when I was on a culinary tour from Atlanta to Miami, I heard about a fish shack about two hours outside of Tampa that was known for its fried grouper sandwich. I'm always willing to do whatever it takes to get the best, most legit version of a regional specialty, whether it's barbecue, fried chicken, or chili—I don't care how far away it is or how long I have to drive to get there. I'm going for it. So, you better believe I made the 100-plus-mile drive to get the fried grouper sandwich that I craved. I was *sooo* hungover from an epic night at Bern's Steak House (a Tampa restaurant famous for its deep, deep cellar and a wine list several hundred pages long), which made the adventure that much trippier.

This recipe is my homage to that seafood-shack sandwich, which was the best I'd ever had. Nothing tastes as good as eating one on the docks looking out on the turquoise waters, but this is close. I don't love a sandwich that's been slathered with too much mayo-laden slaw. It always seems that the mayo is just there to hide sub-par fish. But if you use fresh, beautifully delicate whitefish, you want to elevate it, not hide it. That's why I use sour cream instead of mayonnaise, which makes the sauce tangier and more elegant, like a Danish-style rémoulade. I'm all about the pairing of a fish-shack sandwich with an elevated sauce. It adds so much flavor and moisture to an otherwise boring bun. Juicy fish contrasting the crunch of the fry paired with the buttery buns and the high-acid sauce—what you've got there is a perfect bite.

1 cup all-purpose flour

1 tablespoon kosher salt

½ teaspoon freshly ground black pepper

1 egg

2 tablespoons milk

2 cups panko bread crumbs, or as needed

Four 4-ounce fillets of sole or similar flaky whitefish (see Note)

Neutral oil for frying

Flaky sea salt (such as Maldon)

4 soft hamburger buns

4 teaspoons unsalted butter, at room temperature

Fancy Sauce (recipe follows) for serving

1 lemon, quartered

① Fill a large bowl with the flour, kosher salt, and pepper and stir to combine. In a separate bowl, whisk together the egg and milk. Pour the panko into a third bowl. Line a plate with a double layer of paper towels.

② Working with one piece of fish at a time, dip both sides into the flour, then shake off the excess. Dip into the egg and allow any excess to drip off. Then dip into the panko to coat both sides, pressing to make sure the panko really coats the surface of the fish. (Refresh the panko as needed.)

continued

❸ Fill a Dutch oven or large, heavy-bottomed saucepan with 2 inches of oil and heat to 375°F on a deep-frying thermometer. Working in batches so as not to crowd the pan, gently drop each fillet into the oil and fry until crispy and deeply golden, flipping as needed, 2 to 4 minutes total. Transfer the fish to the prepared plate to drain and then sprinkle with sea salt.

❹ Lightly coat the cut side of each hamburger bun with the butter. In a medium skillet over medium heat, fry the buns until they are golden and toasted, about 1 minute.

❺ Smear some fancy sauce on the bottom buns, then place a fish fillet on each and squeeze a lemon quarter over the tops. Dollop another spoonful of sauce on the fish and close the buns. Serve immediately.

Note: I call for sole here, but any delicate, flaky whitefish will do. Talk to your fishmonger and tell them that you're making a fried-fish sandwich—they'll help you pick out the right variety, just as a sommelier would help you pick out the right wine.

FANCY SAUCE

MAKES ABOUT ¾ CUP

½ cup sour cream

3 tablespoons chopped fresh dill

2 tablespoons chopped dill pickle

2 tablespoons lemon juice

1½ teaspoons hot English mustard

1½ teaspoons jarred grated horseradish

1½ teaspoons kosher salt

1 teaspoon sugar

In a small bowl, combine all the ingredients and stir until incorporated. Store airtight in the fridge for up to 1 week.

CRISPY SHRIMP TACOS

MAKES 12 TACOS

One year for New Year's Eve, my friends and I decided to explore a region of Mexico that I'd never visited: the Valle de Guadalupe and nearby seaside town of Ensenada, both in Baja about two hours south of the US border. I had heard that the Valle had a cool wine scene, and I knew from the countless food shows I'd seen that Ensenada was an amazing seafood town known for its fresh ceviches and fish tacos. I'm very lucky to live in Los Angeles where there are plenty of restaurants that do great, authentic versions of these dishes, but I needed to go to the source.

This recipe is a tribute to that experience as well as to some of my favorite seafood tacos in LA: Ricky's Fish Tacos—a truck where Ricky makes beautifully minimal shrimp tacos with just cabbage slaw, pico, and crema—and La Cevicheria—where you come for the ceviche but never pass up the fried-fish taco plate.

Make sure to use flour, rather than corn, tortillas to stay authentic to the Baja original. The soft suppleness of the flour tortilla is the ideal foil for the crunch of the fried batter.

1 To make the beer batter: In a large bowl, whisk together the flour, mustard, kosher salt, black pepper, cayenne, and baking powder. Slowly pour in the beer and continue whisking until combined. You are looking for a light pancake batter vibe.

2 Fill a Dutch oven or large, heavy-bottomed saucepan with 2 inches of oil and heat to 370°F on a deep-frying thermometer. Line a plate with a double layer of paper towels.

3 Working in batches so as not to crowd the pan, dip the shrimp into the batter and shake off the excess. Gently drop each shrimp into the oil and fry until crispy and deeply golden, flipping as needed, about 3 minutes total. Transfer the shrimp to the prepared plate to drain and then sprinkle with sea salt.

4 If you have a gas range, light one of your burners, or, if you have an electric stove top, set a cast-iron pan over medium heat. Set your tortillas, one at a time, either directly over the flame of your burner or in the cast-iron pan, until they're warm and have a few flecks of char.

5 Place some shrimp and cabbage slaw on a tortilla, then dress with crema, salsa, avocado, cilantro, lots of lime juice, and more sea salt, if needed, before serving.

Beer Batter

1 cup all-purpose flour

1 tablespoon yellow mustard

1 teaspoon kosher salt

1 teaspoon freshly ground black pepper

1 teaspoon cayenne pepper

½ teaspoon baking powder

1 cup light Mexican beer (such as Pacifico)

Neutral oil for frying

1 pound large shrimp, peeled and deveined

Flaky sea salt (such as Maldon)

12 small flour tortillas

Cabbage Slaw (page 36) for serving

Mexican-style crema for serving

Salsa (page 36) for serving

1 avocado, cut into tiny cubes

Cilantro leaves for serving

2 limes, cut into wedges

continued

CABBAGE SLAW

MAKES ABOUT 2 CUPS

½ head small green cabbage, cored and thinly shredded

2 tablespoons lime juice

Kosher salt

In a small bowl, combine the cabbage, lime juice, and ½ teaspoon salt and stir to incorporate. Taste and adjust with more salt if necessary and serve immediately.

SALSA

MAKES ABOUT 1½ CUPS

¾ pound red tomatoes, quartered

¼ white onion, quartered

½ cup cilantro leaves

1 large garlic clove

2 dried chiles de árbol, stemmed (or more, if you want the heat!)

½ red jalapeño or Fresno chile, stemmed but not seeded

1 pinch dried oregano

Kosher salt

In the bowl of a blender, combine the tomatoes, onion, cilantro, garlic, dried chiles, jalapeño, oregano, and ½ teaspoon salt and blend until pureed. Taste and adjust with more salt if necessary. Transfer to the fridge for 1 hour to allow the flavors to meld before using. Store airtight in the fridge for up to 1 week.

Heimy's Hint

It's fun to fry some flour or corn tortillas, cut into chip-size triangles, in the hot oil in between batches of shrimp. Dip in fresh salsa and crema. You're welcome!

AGUACHILE

MAKES 4 SERVINGS

One of my fave Mexican restaurants in LA is Holbox, named after the Yucatán Peninsula's Isla Holbox. The restaurant does this gorg aguachile with a zippy fluorescent/nuclear green miracle sauce. The first time I tasted it, I was perplexed and turned on at the same time. I knew I had to try to re-create it at home.

To really get the bright, radioactive color of the sauce right, you'll need a mortar and pestle; but if you don't have that, chop the herbs and jalapeño as finely as humanly possible. I like to serve this atop tostadas, in honor of another of my favorite LA restaurants, Mariscos Jalisco. If you can't find Fresno chile, substitute red jalapeños.

1 Using a mortar and pestle, pound the cilantro, mint, jalapeño, and ¼ teaspoon salt into a rough paste. Set aside.

2 In a large bowl, combine the shrimp, cucumber, lime juice, and ½ teaspoon salt. Stir to incorporate and allow to marinate until the shrimp is light pink and just starting to turn opaque, 8 to 10 minutes.

3 Add the water to the mortar containing the herb paste and stir to combine.

4 Spoon the shrimp-cucumber mixture in an attractive circle on a serving plate (use a ring mold if you want to get fancy), then pour the green herby mixture evenly over the top. Sprinkle with the Fresno chile, avocado, and red onion and place some pickled serranos (if using) on top. Immediately serve the aguachile with tostadas on the side.

2 tablespoons roughly chopped cilantro

2 tablespoons roughly chopped mint

½ jalapeño chile, seeded (if desired) and chopped

Kosher salt

8 large shrimp, peeled, deveined, and chopped into bite-size pieces

⅓ cup peeled, seeded, and diced (⅛ inch) cucumber

¼ cup lime juice

½ cup water

⅓ cup seeded and diced (⅛ inch) Fresno chile

⅓ cup diced (¼ inch) avocado

1 tablespoon diced (⅛ inch) red onion

Pickled serrano chiles (see page 69), sliced thin (optional)

Tostadas for serving

BAWLMER CRAB CAKE
WITH TANGY TARTAR SAUCE

MAKES 4 CRAB CAKES

1 egg

¼ cup mayonnaise

2 tablespoons chopped fresh parsley

1 tablespoon Dijon mustard

1 tablespoon Worcestershire sauce

1 tablespoon Old Bay Seasoning

1 tablespoon lemon juice

1 tablespoon capers, drained

½ teaspoon kosher salt

1 teaspoon freshly ground black pepper

1 pound high-quality lump crabmeat

⅔ cup cracker crumbs (see Note)

2 tablespoons melted unsalted butter

Tangy Tartar Sauce (recipe follows) for serving

Lemon wedges for serving

Note: To make cracker crumbs, you can use any dry, unflavored cracker (saltines, Ritz crackers, etc.). Simply put the crackers in a ziplock bag and crush them with a mallet, wine bottle, or rolling pin until they are fairly fine with a few coarse crumbs.

I was born in Baltimore, Maryland, so I take crab cakes seriously. Some of my fondest childhood memories are of the steam crab parties we'd throw in the park with my family and neighbors. The newspaper-lined tables, my dad letting me have sips of his beer, the sound of shells cracking, and the pure joy of licking Old Bay from my fingers. Chesapeake Bay blue crab is an international delicacy, and everyone in Baltimore knew it and was extremely proud of it.

My bud Jason Foster, aka the Prince of Baltimore, is another Bawlmer native. A couple of years ago he and I did a 1980s Wall Street–style dinner before our viewing parties of HBO's *Succession*. We'd start with a martini and finish with something era-appropriate, like shrimp cocktail or crab cakes. We sourced really good lump crabmeat and were both surprised by how amazing the cakes turned out with a li'l love.

You have to be light with the seasoning and breading so as not to overpower the delicate blue crabmeat. You can always tell when restaurants are being cheap by skimping on crabmeat and using too many fillers to compensate. These crab cakes are just right, with a hint of Old Bay Seasoning to give that classic Bawlmer flavor. Some deep B'More heads say ANY sauce is sacrilege, but I think it's yum. So FUCK OFF! (That's the Baltimore in me saying that. Peace and Love.)

In the summer, you might be able to find fresh crabmeat—but the rest of the year, you can find jumbo lump crabmeat in a can (I've had good luck with the Handy brand).

The Prince would pair crab cake (or anything, really) with a Bud Light. I would pick a Chenin Blanc from Samur. But we'd both start with a martini.

1 In a large bowl, combine the egg, mayonnaise, parsley, mustard, Worcestershire, Old Bay, lemon juice, capers, salt, and pepper and whisk to incorporate. Add the crab and cracker crumbs and then, using your hands, gently toss everything together, taking care not to break up the larger pieces of crab. Transfer to the refrigerator and chill for 1 hour.

2 Preheat your oven to 450°F. Using a pastry brush, brush a little of the melted butter onto a baking sheet on the area where you will place the crab cakes.

3 Using your hands, gently mold the crab mixture into four hockey puck–size crab cakes. Be careful not to overwork the mixture—it's okay if the patties are a bit loose. Once formed, place them on the prepared baking sheet and paint the tops and sides of the crab cakes with the remaining melted butter.

4 Place the baking sheet in the center of the oven and bake until the crab cakes are lightly browned, about 10 minutes. Remove from the oven.

continued

BAWLMER CRAB CAKE,
CONTINUED

5 Turn on your oven's broiler. Once the broiler is heated, return the baking sheet to the oven and broil for 2 minutes. Keep a close eye on the crab cakes so you don't burn 'em. Once the tops of the crab cakes are nicely browned, remove from the oven.

6 Transfer each crab cake to a plate, top with a dollop of tartar sauce, and serve with lemon wedges on the side.

TANGY TARTAR SAUCE

MAKES ABOUT ½ CUP

¼ cup mayonnaise

1 tablespoon Dijon mustard

1 tablespoon minced red onion

Juice of ½ lemon

½ teaspoon kosher salt

½ teaspoon freshly ground black pepper

In a small bowl, stir together all the ingredients. Store airtight in the fridge for up to 5 days.

THE PRINCE SAYS "NO!" TO CAPERS AND SAUCE

CRAB ROLLS

MAKES 4 SERVINGS

Sushi served omakase-style is one of life's greatest pleasures. *Omakase* translates to "I leave it up to you, chef"—which means the chef will course out a dinner with only the finest and highest-quality fish he has. One of the best meals of my life was a four-hour omakase sushi dinner at restaurant Sawada in Tokyo. I literally cried afterward—I was so moved by the level of care the chef took in preparing everything.

You're never going to be able to re-create that level of sushi experience at home. True sushi masters dedicate their whole lives to their craft. But this is my attempt at honoring one of my favorite parts of an omakase meal. After all the beautiful, subtle fish courses, many chefs finish with a crab hand roll. It is like a savory dessert, a delicious crab tube that basically tells you, "YOU DID IT! You finished the meal!"

The rice is so essential here, and hard to get right. I suggest you invest in a rice cooker, especially if you make rice a lot—it takes out all the guesswork. Regardless of whether you use a rice cooker or not, make sure to buy Japanese short-grain rice, either from a Japanese market or online. While you're there, pick up some nice Japanese nori. Finally, make sure you buy unseasoned rice vinegar (seasoned rice vinegar will be labeled as such and has added sugar, which you don't want). Pair this with very cold dry sake or an Asahi in a frosty glass.

2 cups Japanese short-grain sushi rice

½ cup unseasoned rice vinegar

2 tablespoons sugar

2 teaspoons kosher salt

8 ounces high-quality lump crabmeat (Dungeness works great here)

3 to 4 tablespoons mayonnaise (preferably Kewpie brand)

1 package nori, sheets cut in half

1 avocado, sliced into thin wedges

1 handful bitter microgreens, such as radish or cress

Pickled ginger for serving

Wasabi (fresh, if possible) for serving

Soy sauce for serving

1 Place the rice in a fine-mesh strainer and rinse under cold water, occasionally stirring the rice in the strainer with your hands, until the water runs clear. Then transfer the rice to a bowl and soak in cold water for 30 minutes. Drain the rice.

2 If you're using a rice cooker, add the rice and fresh water according to the manufacturer's instructions. Press the start button and whistle along to the start-up jingle. Thank the appliance gods for this wonderful device. If you don't have a rice cooker, add the rice and 2¼ cups fresh water to a medium, heavy-bottomed pot with a lid and bring to a boil over high heat. Once boiling, cover the pot and turn the heat as low as it will go. Cook for 15 minutes, then remove the pot from the heat and let it rest, covered, until all of the liquid is absorbed and the rice is tender, about 10 minutes more.

3 In the meantime, in a small saucepan over medium-high heat, combine the vinegar, sugar, and salt and cook, stirring, until the sugar and salt are dissolved. Set aside to cool.

4 Now comes the most important step of the sushi rice process—let the rice cool quickly and evenly to maintain the right texture. Spread it out on a baking sheet or in a baking pan in a thin, even layer. Then, use any number of fanning devices—a rice paddle, a mechanical fan, a paper fan; your call—to cool it down. The goal is to stop the rice from steaming. Pause briefly and drizzle about two-thirds of the vinegar mixture evenly over the rice, then,

continued

using a sushi paddle or wooden spoon, gently fold the vinegar evenly into the rice mixture. Taste the rice, add more of the vinegar mixture if you'd like, and go back to fanning until the rice is slightly warmer than room temperature. Transfer to a beautiful serving dish.

5 In a small bowl, combine the crabmeat and mayonnaise (start with 3 tablespoons and add more to taste) and stir gently to incorporate. Transfer to an attractive serving bowl.

6 If your nori isn't super-crisp, you can gently heat it over a medium-low flame on your range. Wave the sheets of nori over the flame in a figure-8 pattern for 15 seconds.

7 Arrange the rice, crab, nori, avocado, microgreens, ginger, wasabi, and soy sauce in small bowls and set on the table. From there, everybody should make their own hand rolls by scooping a spoonful of rice and spreading it along one of the narrow edges of the nori. Top the rice with a spoonful of crab, then with the avocado and microgreens and roll into a loose cylinder. Dip in soy sauce, if desired, and enjoy with the ginger and wasabi on the side.

SPICE-SO-NICE CHEESY EGGWICH DELUXE

MAKES 4 SANDWICHES

It's important to incorporate circles into every meal of the day. This led me to the concept of the "Heimy BoB" (Breakfast on a Bun). Inspired by the McMuffins of my childhood, and the bacon, egg, and cheese sandwiches that I used to buy from trucks in college in Philly, this BoB is elevated in every possible way. Griddled brioche bun. The freshest farmers' market eggs. Perfect, in-season heirloom tomatoes. Smoked bacon. To fry my eggs, I like to crack them into a buttered ring mold or the buttered lid of a wide-mouth mason jar to ensure that they are perfectly circular. If you're serious about reaching circle-food nirvana, you've gotta be willing to go that extra mile.

4 slices smoked bacon

¼ cup unsalted butter

4 brioche buns

4 eggs

Kosher salt and freshly ground black pepper

4 slices sharp cheddar

¼ cup mayonnaise

1 tablespoon Tabasco sauce

4 slices heirloom tomato

1 Preheat your oven to 400°F. Line a baking sheet with aluminum foil. Line a plate with a double layer of paper towels.

2 Lay the bacon on the baking sheet and bake until golden brown and crispy, about 20 minutes. Transfer to the prepared plate to drain.

3 Set a skillet over medium heat and add 1 tablespoon of the butter. Add the buns cut-side down and toast, about 30 seconds. Set aside.

4 Add the remaining 3 tablespoons butter to the skillet and, working in batches as needed, crack the eggs directly into the skillet or into buttered 3½-inch ring molds set in the skillet, then sprinkle with salt and pepper. Fry to your desired doneness. I like mine over-easy, which means I cook them for about 1½ minutes, until the bottom starts to set, then I cover the pan with a lid or plate (to help the egg white cook through) and cook for 1 minute more. Using a butter knife to loosen the edges, remove the ring molds and carefully flip each egg, add a slice of the cheese, re-cover the pan, and cook just until the cheese has melted, about 30 seconds.

5 In a small bowl, mix together the mayonnaise and Tabasco.

6 Smear some of the spicy sauce on the cut sides of each bun, then place a tomato slice on the bottom bun and season with salt. Top with a cheesy egg, then break the bacon into pieces and place atop the cheesy egg. Finally, top with the other half of the bun and serve.

Like most kids, I was obsessed with pizza. And, like most kids who grew up in the 1980s, it started with Pizza Hut. There was something magical about those buttery pan pizzas. My friends and I would save up all the change we could find—on the street, in between couch cushions—and when we'd amassed enough, we'd hop on our BMX bikes and ride down to the local Pizza Hut. This was a big deal because it was our first restaurant outing without our parents, which meant we got to do adult stuff, like figuring out how to tip or how to befriend the manager so we'd get free breadsticks. Those early Pizza Hut experiences were about more than just pepperoni pan pizzas, fountain Cokes in red plastic cups with pellet ice, and buttery breadsticks. They were about freedom.

From Pizza Hut we graduated to Tony's Pizza, a local spot in my hometown of Audubon, Pennsylvania. We'd drop our bikes ('cause kickstands were lame) out front and head inside, where Mimmo (the first real pizzaiolo I ever encountered) would toss a seventy-five-cent slice of pizza into the back of the deck oven to reheat to perfect crispiness. (Maybe that's where my love for crisp comes from—that wonderful reheated slice experience.) We never actually ordered a full, fresh pie, because we didn't have the money. Next step was to douse that slice with garlic salt, red pepper flakes, and shaker Parmesan until you could barely see the mozzarella. Mimmo was cool. He barely spoke English, had prison tats, and let us smoke inside.

To me, one of the beauties of pizza is the communal aspect, the idea of everyone going in on one pie and grabbing a piece. I love making it at home with friends. Everyone gathers around as I stretch out the dough and add the toppings. We collectively hold our breath as I transfer the pizza from the peel into the oven—will it land on the stone in a perfect circle?! When it does, I yell "HERE WE GO!" and we cheer. As the pie bakes, we smell the raw dough transforming into this beautifully baked crust. When it comes out and the cheese is perfectly melted, the crust has bubbles and air pockets from fermentation and flecks of char, when we all know it was a good bake, we literally erupt into song and dance: "It's Pie Time, darlin'! It's Pie Time, okay!" Then we bite into slices hot from the oven, when the cheese is still oozing and the crust is warm and chewy in exactly the right way. That's the beauty of pizza night: the sense of togetherness, of sharing those perfect bites with the people you care about. It's a magical thing.

With a lot of things, your tastes change as you get older. But my love for pizza never went away—it just grew and grew. Then I visited pizza's birthplace, Italy, for the first time, and my love became a full-blown obsession. Eating pizza in Napoli is basically a religious experience. You look up and you see Mount Vesuvius—an active volcano!—and realize that the best tomatoes in the world, San Marzano tomatoes, are literally grown in its shadow. As with wine, the volcanic soils influence the terroir of those tomatoes, which is part of why they are so insane and unlike any other tomatoes on Earth. Then there's the cheese, which either comes from the region or is trucked in from Puglia. Some of the best pizza spots in Rome and Naples send a driver to Puglia every night to bring in the freshest burrata and mozzarella. These guys are serious about cheese!

These are just two of the reasons why Neapolitan-style pizza is in a class by itself. Italians have been farming this land and making these products for thousands of years. In some cases, the same family has been growing tomatoes or making cheese in the same place for centuries. They have such a deep understanding and awareness of their food heritage. This is why their approach to food, especially pizza, is one of simplicity and restraint. It's just like sushi: It's all about the quality of your ingredients and their proportions. There's a balance of fish to rice, and there's a balance of sauce to dough. Why would you load up a pizza with a ton of toppings when you're working with the best tomatoes and cheese on the planet? You want to let those ingredients shine through.

Napoli-style pizza is its own special thing, but there's also an amazing array of American pizzas that I love dearly. I've reflected a lot on what blows me away when it comes to American pizza, and I've realized that it's a hybrid style. To me, the five pizza spots that define the American approach are Frank Pepe Pizzeria Napoletana in New Haven, Di Fara Pizza in Brooklyn, Pizzeria Bianco in Phoenix, Pizzeria Beddia in Philly, and Pequod's Pizza in Chicago. Each of these places does pizza a little bit differently, but they've all influenced my pizza philosophy. I love that they each interpret the Italian tradition in a different way to make it work on their home turf.

When I set out to master pizza-making at home, I knew I wanted something inspired by all of these different pizza styles. Mix a li'l New York, a li'l Philly, a li'l Bianco, sprinkle in some pizzazz, and you've got HEIMY PIES!

On a practical level, I wanted to develop an approach that works for me and my home kitchen in Los Angeles. I am working with a standard home oven that gets up to about 575°F or so (I'm blessed with an oven that runs pretty hot), not 900°F like wood-fired pizza ovens. I'm also working with unique climate conditions—humidity and temperature affect dough development, so I have to adapt to my environment.

In the next couple of pages, I share my approach to making pizza in my home kitchen. But you will have to practice and pay attention and adjust my approach to work for you and your kitchen. Maybe—probably—you live somewhere colder than Los Angeles, which means your dough might take a little longer to ferment. Maybe your oven runs cooler than mine, and your pizzas need to bake a bit longer. Maybe your oven has a hot spot on the bottom and the crust cooks before the cheese melts, which means you need to play around with the broiler to get a nice char on the top. (Don't be afraid of some burned bits. Crispy Life is Good Life!)

I've offered some troubleshooting advice on page 65, but my main advice is to just keep Zah'n! Take notes about each pizza bake so you can make adjustments the next time. Don't get discouraged. Pizzaiolos are craftsmen. The greatest pizzaiolos are artists. I'm still honing my craft, and I get better with every pie. You will too.

Heimy's Hint

When trying a new pizza spot, I ALWAYS start with their margherita pie. This way I can really get a feel for the crust, sauce, and cheese. A supreme pie is a no-no for me.

MY PIZZA EVOLUTION

- **A** Pizza Hut (Audubon, PA)
- **B** Tony's Pizza (Audubon, PA)
- **C** Pizzeria da Attilio (Naples, Italy)
- **D** Bonci (Rome, Italy)
- **E** Frank Pepe Pizzeria Napoletana (New Haven, CT)
- **F** Di Fara Pizza (Brooklyn)
- **G** Pizzeria Bianco (Phoenix)
- **H** Pizzeria Beddia (Philadelphia)
- **I** Pequod's Pizza (Chicago)
- **J** Tony's Pizza Napoletana (San Francisco)
- **K** Pizzeria Mozza (Los Angeles)

My Favorite American Pies

My first encounter with New Haven–style pizza was when Jon Mugar, our tour manager, diverted our tour bus many hours because he insisted we experience this charred greatness. This is one of the oldest American styles of pizza: It began in Connecticut in the early 1900s, when Italian immigrants started baking pizzas in coal- and coke-fired bread ovens. (Coke is converted coal and burns super-hot.) Some called it "apizza," others called it "tomato pie," I guess to make it sound less scary and "foreign" to Americans. **Frank Pepe** was founded in 1925, and what they call a "pizza napoletana" is a thin, super-crispy and blistered crust with a beautiful char on the bottom. That is 100 percent New Haven–style. Don't skip the clam pie. Trust Heim. Chef's Bow.

Di Fara offers your classic New York pie. This is the style most of us grew up eating and has become the ubiquitous "American style" pie: cooked directly on the hearth of a deck oven (rather than in a pan, like the Detroit or Chicago styles) at temperatures between 550° and 650°F. The lower temp means New York pizzas bake for much longer than Neapolitan wood-fired pizzas, resulting in a crisper, less squishy crust. Low-moisture mozzarella, as opposed to fresh styles such as fior di latte, is another signature of New York pies and results in that long, stretchy cheese pull. Di Fara creates everything I dream of in a New York pie: crisp crust, a combo of low-moisture and fresh mozz, scissor-cut basil, and a big dose of olive oil to finish. Plus it's in the tiniest, vibiest spot in Brooklyn. My friends did not understand why I made us wait for an hour just to grab a pie, but once inside and watching the master, Dom DeMarco, lovingly drizzle olive oil over his pizza canvas, they got it. True beauty.

My first experience with a **Bianco** pie was through my good friend Amanny Ahmad. Knowing how much I adore Zah, she flew a Rosa pizza home with her from Phoenix, then brought it directly to my house from the airport to inspect. Even at room temp, I could appreciate the beautiful simplicity and extreme flavor goodness I was dealing with. I was instantly hooked. Then I met the man. Chris Bianco is basically my all-around life guru. It would take an entire book to explain what he does for me and the world with his gentle spirit and masterful skills. Being in his presence, you get an insight into his philosophies just by the way he tells a story about his dad's paintings, which hang in his restaurant. Or his love for the farmers who deliver to him beautiful fruit every day. The way he explains his techniques and ingredients—like grain and tomatoes from different parts of America—is so inspiring and connects you to the food in a very real way. And his general "screw the noise, eat the real shit" attitude is infectious. Then there're his pizzas . . . they're goddamn masterpieces. I was lucky

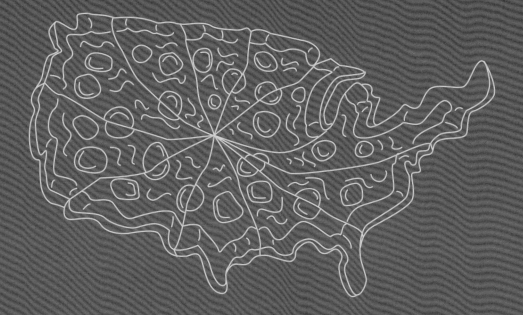

enough to absorb his pizza teachings in many different settings, using different ingredients and types of ovens. But it's all the same to him. Quality, time, patience, and, most important, DELICIOUSNESS.

In my hometown of Philly, Joe **Beddia** uses an aged gouda as a substitute for Parmigiano-Reggiano. This would be sacrilege in Napoli, but it gives an amazing creaminess and unique texture to his pies. He has a similar approach as Di Fara but uses really, really good ingredients that make eating his pies a heavenly experience. We have bonded over Howard Stern and chirashi bowls and have traveled the world together in search of premium bites and mind-blowing sips. He's a special boy and my soul sister who is equal parts sushi master and dim bulb. He also helped come up with brilliant alternate titles to this book (see page 59).

Pequod's is a whole other pizza dimension: deep dish on steroids (if steroids were an injection of crispy, caramelized, cheesy crust magic). Deep dish pizza is baked in a round, cast-iron pan, rather than directly on the hearth of an oven. The dough is slightly different too; it's enriched with oil so it's sturdier and can hold the weight of all the toppings, which are inverted—cheese first, then tomato sauce, then the rest. I have never been to Chicago without getting a pie from Pequod's, where they layer slices of mozzarella all the way to the edge of the pan. The cheese that comes in contact with the pan will blister as it bakes and form this beautiful, crispy crust. They say that after one slice, you're done. But before shows when I'm on tour in Chicago, I always eat two. It's my tradition and I can't resist. After Pizza Hut, this is the main inspiration for my Personal Pan Pep Pep (page 86).

JOE BEDDIA'S ALTERNATE TITLES FOR THIS BOOK

CONSIDER THE FOODIE

HOW TO COOK A SQUIRREL

BREAK EGGS NOT BUTTS

BITES + SIPS + JUICY LIPS

CHEZ WAREHEIM

EAT FUN #1

CULINARY SWEET NOTHINGS

ERIC WAREHEIM FOOD ARTIST

BIGFOOT CONTESSA

PIZZA DOUGH

MAKES ENOUGH FOR SIX 12- TO 14-INCH PIZZAS

650 grams / 2¾ cups 70°F
filtered water

1 kilogram / 7 cups
bread flour

50 grams / ¼ cup
extra-virgin olive oil

30 grams / 2 tablespoons
plus 1 teaspoon packed
brown sugar

2 grams / ⅔ teaspoon
instant dried yeast

20 grams / 2 tablespoons
kosher salt

Semolina flour for sprinkling

There's something so epic about making pizza at home. When you pull your first pie out of the oven, nothing beats that moment of I MADE A FREAKING PIZZA PIE IN MY HOME! I AM A PIZZA CHAMPION!

I developed this recipe with the help of my dough bro Noel Brohner of Slow Rise Pizza, a legend and international pizza consultant/fixer who teaches home pizza-making classes in Los Angeles. Besides being a pizza master, he's a very inspirational teacher and a solid, premium-level friend. We were aiming for the perfect hybrid dough: something that blends the best characteristics of Neapolitan- and New York–style pizzas, with a deeply flavorful crust and a beautiful crumb that is delicate yet won't flop over when you pick it up to take a bite. This dough is specifically developed to deliver great pies from your kitchen's oven.

Instead of 00 flour, which is traditional in Neapolitan pizzas, we use bread flour (also known as baker's flour), and we hydrate the dough with water and olive oil. This makes the dough a bit more elastic and easier to work with. It's forgiving as you stretch and shape it, which means you can make a bigger pie and you don't have to stress about rips and tears. Plus, the pie doesn't get as goopy in the middle as a Neapolitan pizza does.

I make my dough in a stand mixer fitted with the dough hook attachment. The machine does all the work of kneading. If you don't have a stand mixer at home, I've also included a variation for mixing by hand, which is fun and kinda primal. You can halve the recipe if you want, but I love having a bit of extra dough to play with, even if it's just to make a simple flatbread (see page 70).

❶ In the bowl of a stand mixer fitted with the dough hook attachment, add the water and then the flour, olive oil, and brown sugar. Mix at the lowest speed setting for 3½ minutes, scraping down the sides of the bowl as necessary, until the ingredients are well incorporated. Turn off the mixer and let the dough rest for 20 minutes.

❷ Add the yeast to the mixture and mix for 1 minute at the lowest speed setting, then add the salt and mix for 1 minute more. Turn the speed to the next setting and mix for an additional 4 minutes. Do the "windowpane test" to check the dough's gluten development: Pull a small piece of dough and stretch it up between your fingers. You should be able to stretch it so that it becomes translucent (like a windowpane) with threads of gluten visible without the dough ripping. If it rips, mix for another minute or two to develop the gluten further.

❸ Lightly oil a plastic dough bin or large bowl and gently transfer the dough into it, using a plastic dough scraper to assist. Cover with the lid or plastic wrap and allow to rest for 30 minutes.

❹ Time for the first stretch and fold! Lightly oil your hands, then grab about a third of the dough mass, pull it up and away, and fold it over the top of the dough. Spin the tub or bowl 180 degrees and repeat the process. Repeat

continued

twice more for four total folds, so your dough looks like a nice li'l package. Flip the whole mass of dough upside down so the exposed top is smooth and round.

5 Cover the dough and let rest for another 30 minutes. Then repeat the whole "stretch and fold" process again. Now re-cover the dough and place the whole thing in the refrigerator overnight to ferment and develop flavor. Just like Heimy, this dough needs at least 8 hours of beauty sleep.

6 The next day, remove the dough from the refrigerator 4 hours before you plan to bake the pizzas and allow to rest, covered, at room temperature for 30 minutes.

7 Generously flour the dough tub or a baking sheet where you will be storing your finished dough balls. Tip the dough out onto a clean, floured work surface. Cut the dough into six equal portions. (Each ball should weigh just shy of 300 grams.)

8 Time to ball! Flour your hands and grab a piece of dough. Knock off any excess flour from the bottom. Begin to fold the sides underneath the dough mass, pinching the seams closed at the bottom as you go. You're sort of stretching and creating surface tension on the dough by pulling the top and tucking it under. It's a little tricky at first but you'll get the hang of it. The goal is to create a smooth uniform ball with a tightly closed seam underneath. Place each shaped ball into the prepared tub or onto the baking sheet. Be sure to leave a couple of inches of space between the balls, because they will grow. Then either close the lid or flour the tops of the dough balls and cover the baking sheet with plastic wrap. Let the balls rest until they're about one and a half times their original size, about 4 hours.

9 Flour a clean kitchen counter or large cutting board. Sprinkle your pizza peel with semolina. Flour your hands and, using a dough scraper, very gently transfer the dough ball to the prepared surface.

10 Using your fingertips and starting in the center of the dough, lightly push down and outward to start to form a round shape. I like to leave the outer ½-inch edge untouched so it will form a nice and puffy crust. Once you've expanded the dough to a pillowy, 7-inch disk, carefully pick it up and drape it over your fists. Gravity will begin to stretch the edges of the dough. Move your fists around, slowly stretching and pulling to make a circle. I like to alternate between this technique and placing the disk on the surface to continue stretching it there. The goal is a perfect circle 12 to 14 inches in diameter with a very even thickness.

11 Once you've formed your crust, transfer it to the pizza peel and dress the pizza according to the recipe.

12 Right before you bake, give the crust one extra stretch by sliding your fingers under the dough near the edges, about ½ inch in, and give it a couple of tugs to stretch it evenly on all sides. This will ensure a perfectly even crust thickness.

Variation

To mix by hand, place the flour in a large bowl and make a well in the center. Add the olive oil, brown sugar, and about half of the water to the well. Start incorporating flour from the side into the center of the well. Spin the bowl as you work and continue to move flour from the edges of the bowl into the center of the well. Every now and then, work the dough mass in the center of the bowl by kind of aggressively massaging and squeezing it in between your fingers, to incorporate all the ingredients.

After about 1 minute, when you feel like the water is evenly integrated into the flour, add about half of the remaining water and continue to incorporate it into the dough. After another 3 minutes of mixing, add the last of the water and mix for 2 minutes longer, until all the ingredients are well integrated and the dough is a tacky but cohesive mass.

Cover the bowl with a damp towel and let it rest for 5 minutes. Then add the yeast and mix for 1 minute. Add the salt and mix for 3 minutes more. Let rest, covered with the towel, for 5 minutes.

After the 5 minutes of rest, wet both of your hands and pick up the entire dough mass. Fold it in half upon itself, like you're closing a book, then rotate the dough mass and fold it upon itself again. Repeat this folding process for 1 minute—you'll feel the dough start to stiffen up. Let the dough rest, covered, for 5 minutes, then repeat the folding process for 1 minute more. This time, transfer the dough to a lightly oiled dough bin or bowl, cover with a lid, or plastic and let rest for 10 minutes. Then continue as directed with the first stretch and fold (see step 4).

USE YOUR HANDS

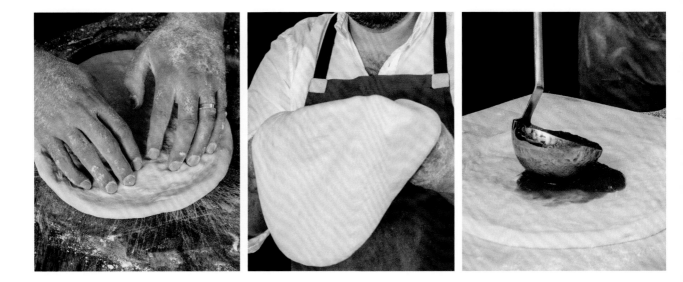

TROUBLESHOOTING PIZZA

Q: My dough is rising way faster/slower than the recipe instructions say.

A: The pizza dough recipe assumes that you're working in an environment with an ambient temperature of 70°F. Heat speeds up fermentation, so if it's hotter than 70°F in your kitchen, use water that is slightly colder than 70°F to slow things down at the beginning. For the bulk fermentation and dough rise, consider moving the dough bins to a cooler, dark room or closet. If it's significantly colder than 70°F in your kitchen, then fermentation will be slower. Start with warmer water and move your dough bins or dough balls to a sunny window to speed things up.

Q: My pizza keeps getting stuck on the pizza peel!

A: Make sure to dust that peel with enough semolina flour. Also, don't let the dressed pizza sit on the peel for too long before you transfer it to the oven. If you do need to wait before it goes into the oven, give the peel a shake every once in a while. You should load it up on the peel and add the toppings right before you're going to put it in the oven.

Q: My pizzas are taking way longer to cook than your instructions say!

A: Every oven is different, and yours might not get as hot as mine. Every time you open the oven door, you lose heat, so wait a couple of minutes in between pizzas to let it come back up to temperature. Also, some ovens heat from the bottom, and some heat from the top. Arrange your oven rack so it's as close to the heat source as possible. If you can't get your oven up to 550°F, you might have to cook the pie for a minute or two longer than the instructions say.

Q: My pizza is soggy in the middle!

A: You over-cheesed or over-sauced. You really want about 4 ounces of cheese on a 12-inch pizza, otherwise you'll weigh it down. And since every dough is different—sometimes it's super-elastic and you get a big pie, sometimes it's a bit tighter and you might end up with a smaller pie—you should use your best judgment when it comes time to add the sauce. Don't be alarmed if you end up using a bit less than the recipe calls for.

FRESH RED SAUCE

MAKES ABOUT 3 CUPS

One 28-ounce can whole tomatoes (see Note)

3 garlic cloves, finely minced

1½ tablespoons extra-virgin olive oil

1½ teaspoons kosher salt

2 basil leaves

The San Marzano tomatoes that grow in Campania, Italy, are some of the best in the world; just incredible li'l zingy flavor bombs. This is why pizzaiolos in Napoli keep things really simple when it comes to sauce—a little salt, maybe a bit of olive oil, that's it—to preserve the incredible, bright flavors of the tomatoes. No cooking involved, which really allows the raw tomato flavor to sing. Make a double-batch and freeze some for whenever you want a quick pasta lunch.

❶ Run the tomatoes through a food mill (best) or squeeze them with your hands (okay); you want them to be crushed but not a totally smooth puree. They should have a little body and be very spreadable (not thin and watery). Transfer to a bowl and stir in the garlic, olive oil, salt, and basil.

❷ Transfer to the refrigerator and let chill for 2 hours to allow the flavors to meld before using. If not using right away, store airtight in the fridge for up to 1 week or in the freezer for up to 3 months.

Note: If you open the can of tomatoes and there is a thin, watery layer of juice on top, pour it off and set it aside. After you crush the tomatoes, add back a little bit of the tomato water to achieve the desired consistency.

COOKED RED SAUCE

MAKES ABOUT 3 CUPS

One 28-ounce can whole tomatoes

1 tablespoon extra-virgin olive oil

4 anchovy fillets

3 garlic cloves, finely minced

1½ teaspoons red pepper flakes

Kosher salt

The Fresh Red Sauce above is really vibrant but delicate, basically a blank canvas for other pizza toppings. This cooked sauce has a bit more of an assertive flavor. It's naughty. And when you're feeling naughty, you sometimes crave a danker sauce. It's great on a pie with punchy flavors, like my Caperberry Pie (page 77).

❶ Run the tomatoes through a food mill (best) or squeeze them with your hands (okay); you want them to be crushed but not a totally smooth puree. They should have a little body and be very spreadable (not thin and watery).

❷ In a medium saucepan over medium heat, warm the olive oil, then add the anchovies and garlic and cook until the anchovies break down, 1 to 2 minutes. Add the tomatoes, red pepper flakes, and ¾ teaspoon salt and turn the heat to a simmer. Cook until the flavors have melded, about 3 minutes. Taste and adjust the seasoning as needed. If not using right away, store airtight in the fridge for up to 1 week or in the freezer for up to 2 months.

PEPPER CREAM

MAKES ABOUT 2½ CUPS

This cream sauce is gonna make your kitchen smell so damn good and get you VERY excited for your pizza party. When friends come over, their eyes will dilate from the garlic and shallot aromas. Pass around the wine, and get ready to ZAH. When you're mixing this, stop when it's nice and spreadable and not too runny. Somewhere in between Alfredo sauce thickness and Cool Whip thickness.

2 tablespoons extra-virgin olive oil

2 shallots, very thinly sliced

4 garlic cloves, minced

1 cup heavy whipping cream

½ teaspoon kosher salt

¼ teaspoon freshly ground white pepper

1 In a medium saucepan over medium-low heat, warm the olive oil, then add the shallots and cook until translucent, 1 to 2 minutes. Add the garlic, cooking just until fragrant, about 30 seconds more. Don't burn the garlic! (If it starts to smell bitter, toss it out and start over.) Remove the shallot-garlic mixture from the heat and allow to cool to room temperature.

2 Pour the cream into a bowl and whisk vigorously until it has thickened slightly, about 5 minutes. Stop when the cream forms very soft peaks. Stir in the cooled shallot-garlic mixture and season with the salt and white pepper. If not using right away, store airtight in the fridge for up to 2 days.

ROSEMARY-CHILE OIL

MAKES ABOUT ½ CUP

Welcome to Drizzle Town. This spicy oil will kick up any damn dish, but especially flatbread (see page 70) or focaccia.

Don't forget to re-up your spice rack. If your red pepper flakes are old as hell and have moved with you to several different apartments or houses, then you should throw them out and buy new ones or your oil will be less spicy and vibrant. Fresh, high-quality pepper flakes will make your oil taste better and give you that nutso bold red color.

½ cup extra-virgin olive oil

2 tablespoons red pepper flakes

1 teaspoon whole black peppercorns

1 sprig rosemary

1 whole dried Calabrian chile (optional)

1 In a saucepan over medium-low heat, warm the olive oil, then add the red pepper flakes, peppercorns, and rosemary and cook for 5 minutes. Remove from the heat and let the mixture steep for at least 2 hours—or longer! (The longer you steep, the spicier the oil, so keep tasting until you reach a level you like.)

2 When you've achieved your preferred spice level, strain and discard the solids. Transfer the oil to a glass bottle or storage container and add the chile (for cuteness). Store at room temperature for up to 1 month.

QUICKLE PICKLE

MAKES ABOUT 1 PINT

EMBRACE ACID!

Sour—whether it comes from a squeeze of fresh lemon or a drizzle of vinegar—is one of the most important and underrated flavors out there.

Whenever I taste a dish and feel as though something is missing, nine times out of ten, acid is the answer. That's when I reach for a quick-pickled vegetable. Think about a fried chicken sandwich. You have the sweetness of the bun, savoriness of the meat, and fattiness of the fry. Without acid, it's unbalanced, and kind of a gut bomb. But add a quick-pickled cucumber or red onion, and, suddenly, that baby is singing high notes.

This is my basic pickle recipe, and you can use it for any vegetable: chiles, cucumbers, carrots, cauliflower, onions. You can add spices or herbs if you'd like: dill with cucumbers, coriander with carrots, turmeric with cauliflower. Experiment, and soon you will be an acid freak like me. Once you've pickled some serrano or Fresno chiles and added them to a cheesy pie, you will crave that dynamic forever.

1 cup white vinegar

1 tablespoon kosher salt

1 tablespoon sugar

8 ounces vegetables of your choice (chiles, cucumbers, carrots, cauliflower, and onions are all good)

1 In a small saucepan over medium heat, combine the vinegar, salt, and sugar and stir until the salt and sugar are dissolved. Remove from the heat and let cool to room temperature.

2 Scrub clean your vegetables and peel if necessary. Cut them into ⅛-inch slices and pack them tightly into a clean 1-pint mason jar or other storage container. Pour the cooled vinegar mixture over the top. If necessary, add some water to ensure the vegetables are submerged.

3 Your pickles will be ready to use after 1 hour. If not using right away, store airtight in the fridge for up to 2 weeks.

FLATBREAD
WITH OLIVES AND SEMIDRIED TOMATOES

MAKES ONE 12- TO 14-INCH FLATBREAD

1 ball Pizza Dough (page 60)

Semolina flour for sprinkling

¼ cup extra-virgin olive oil

¼ cup olives, pitted and torn into pieces

¼ cup semidried tomatoes

Freshly grated Pecorino for finishing

Flaky sea salt (such as Maldon)

Rosemary-Chile Oil (page 67) for serving

I always make a flatbread before my friends come over so they can have snackers as soon as they arrive. There's nothing worse than a dinner party with no snick-snacks! This recipe is no-frills and all about respecting the raw elements and purity of the dough. Something to get your palate excited for the feast to come. No melted cheese, no sauce—just delicious olives and tomatoes. Buy good olives in brine and pit them yourself; pitted olives are always inferior. And look for semidried tomatoes at an Italian specialty food store. They still have some juiciness to them. They're sold packed in oil in jars.

1 One hour before you plan to make the flatbread, place your pizza stone on the bottom rack of your oven and preheat to 550°F (or, if the oven won't get that hot, as hot as it will go). This will superheat the pizza stone.

2 Shape the dough as instructed in steps 9 and 10 on page 62. Use a fork to poke holes all over the surface. This is to prevent the flatbread from puffing up too much (usually a pizza's cheese and toppings prevent this from happening).

3 Using both hands, transfer the dough to the prepared pizza peel. If the dough gets misshapen during the transfer, don't worry, just nudge it back into the shape of a circle. Grab the peel by the handle and flick your wrist to shake it back and forth a bit, to ensure the dough isn't stuck to the peel.

4 Drizzle 2 tablespoons of the olive oil evenly over the surface of the dough. Use your fingers or a pastry brush to make sure it's evenly coated.

5 Working quickly to maintain the oven's temperature, transfer the dough from the peel to the stone. To do this, angle the pizza peel at about 45 degrees with the edge touching the back of the stone. The dough should slide off the peel and make contact with the back of the stone. Swiftly pull away the peel and the dough should land in a tidy circle on the stone.

6 Cook for 3 minutes, then, using the peel, remove the flatbread from the oven. Dress the flatbread by scattering the olives and tomatoes evenly over the surface. Return the flatbread to the oven and cook until golden brown, an additional 1 to 2 minutes.

7 Using the peel, remove the flatbread from the oven. Drizzle with the remaining 2 tablespoons olive oil, then finish with a sprinkle of Pecorino and sea salt.

8 Cut the flatbread into 2-inch squares and serve with the rosemary-chile oil on the side.

CHEESEHEIM

MAKES ONE 12- TO 14-INCH PIZZA

The CheeseHeim is my pride and joy. It looks simple but it requires finesse. If you overload it with too much sauce or cheese, you'll end up with a sad, soggy middle. Not cute! Remember, less is more. The Heimy touch is to add a handful of roasted cherry tomatoes along with the tomato sauce, to kick things up a notch. Two kinds of tomatoes. Two kinds of mozzarellas. Four layers of happiness!

1 One hour before you plan to make the pizza, place your pizza stone on the bottom rack of your oven and preheat to 550°F (or, if the oven won't get that hot, as hot as it will go). This will superheat the pizza stone.

2 Shape the dough as instructed in steps 9 and 10 on page 62.

3 Using both hands, transfer the dough to the prepared pizza peel. If the dough gets misshapen during the transfer, nudge it back into the shape of a circle. Grab the peel by the handle and flick your wrist to shake it back and forth a bit, to ensure the dough isn't stuck to the peel.

4 Using a ladle, spoon the sauce into the center of the dough and then spiral it out toward the edges with the back of the ladle, leaving a ½-inch rim around the edge. Distribute the low-moisture mozz evenly over the sauce. Place the fior di latte evenly over the pie. Not too much! And none in the center of the pie, please. Then sprinkle the roasted tomatoes over the top and drizzle a bit of olive oil over everything.

5 Working quickly to maintain the oven's temperature, transfer the pizza from the peel to the stone. To do this, angle the pizza peel at about 45 degrees with the edge touching the back of the stone. The pizza should slide off the peel and make contact with the back of the stone. Swiftly pull away the peel and the pizza should land in a tidy circle on the stone.

6 Cook for 3½ minutes, then, using the peel, rotate the pizza 180 degrees to ensure even cooking and cook for 2½ minutes more. The cheese should be melted and there should be flecks of char on the crust.

7 Using the peel, remove the pie from the oven. Top with the fresh basil, salt, and a touch more olive oil, then finish with a sprinkle of Parm and oregano. Serve immediately.

---

1 Preheat your oven to 400°F.

2 Drizzle the olive oil on the bottom of a baking sheet, then arrange the tomatoes on the sheet. Season with salt, then roast for 10 minutes. Store airtight in the fridge for up to 5 days—they're great on top of scrambled eggs or toast.

1 ball Pizza Dough (page 60)

Semolina flour for sprinkling

½ cup Fresh Red Sauce (page 66), or as needed

⅓ cup shredded low-moisture mozzarella

½ cup bite-size pieces fior di latte fresh whole-milk mozzarella, drained on paper towels

1 handful Roasted Tomatoes (recipe follows)

Extra-virgin olive oil for drizzling

1 handful fresh basil leaves, torn

1 pinch kosher salt

Freshly grated Parmigiano-Reggiano for finishing

Dried oregano for finishing

ROASTED TOMATOES

MAKES ABOUT ½ CUP

2 tablespoons extra-virgin olive oil

1 pint cherry tomatoes, halved

Kosher salt

QUEEN MADI'S POTATO PIE

MAKES ONE 12- TO 14-INCH PIZZA

2 medium creamer potatoes (such as red or Yukon gold)

2 tablespoons extra-virgin olive oil, plus more for drizzling

Kosher salt

1 ball Pizza Dough (page 60)

Semolina flour for sprinkling

½ cup Pepper Cream (page 67), or as needed

¾ cup shredded low-moisture mozzarella

1 teaspoon fresh rosemary

Freshly ground black pepper

Freshly grated Parmigiano-Reggiano for finishing

This pie is a brainchild of my queen, Madi, and I love it. Usually I say nish to starch on starch, but the way she prepares it, with super-thin potatoes roasted to perfection, it's really a stunner. Side note: Madi grew up IN a pizza restaurant, literally, so she knows what she is talking about. This is a next-level circular experience.

1. Preheat your oven to 400°F.

2. Slice the potatoes ⅛ inch thick. (A mandoline is great for this.) Drizzle the 2 tablespoons olive oil on the bottom of a baking sheet, then arrange the potatoes on the sheet. Season with salt and then roast until golden around the edges but not crispy, 10 minutes. Set aside.

3. One hour before you plan to make the pizza, place your pizza stone on the bottom rack of your oven and preheat to 550°F (or, if the oven won't get that hot, as hot as it will go). This will superheat the pizza stone.

4. Shape the dough as instructed in steps 9 and 10 on page 62.

5. Using both hands, transfer the dough to the prepared pizza peel. If the dough gets misshapen during the transfer, nudge it back into the shape of a circle. Grab the peel by the handle and flick your wrist to shake it back and forth a bit, to ensure the dough isn't stuck to the peel.

6. Using a ladle, spoon the cream into the center of the dough and then spiral it out toward the edges with the back of the ladle, leaving a ½-inch rim around the edge. Sprinkle half of the mozz over the cream, then arrange the potato slices neatly on top, overlapping the edges a bit. Sprinkle the rosemary over the potatoes, then distribute the rest of the mozz. Sprinkle with a few cranks of black pepper.

7. Working quickly to maintain the oven's temperature, transfer the pizza from the peel to the stone. To do this, angle the pizza peel at about 45 degrees with the edge touching the back of the stone. The pizza should slide off the peel and make contact with the back of the stone. Swiftly pull away the peel and the pizza should land in a tidy circle on the stone.

8. Cook for 3½ minutes, then, using the peel, rotate the pizza 180 degrees to ensure even cooking and cook for 2½ minutes more. The cheese should be melted and there should be flecks of char on the crust.

9. Using the peel, remove the pie from the oven. Finish with a pinch of salt, some Parm, and a spiraling drizzle of olive oil. Serve immediately.

CAPERBERRY PIE

MAKES ONE 12- TO 14-INCH PIZZA

You may be familiar with capers, the teeny, briny flavor bombs you eat on a bagel with lox. Those are actually the pickled buds of the caper plant, whereas caperberries are the big boys: the fully grown fruit, pickled. Slice 'em up to get that bright, saline flavor that contrasts beautifully with the creamy cheese.

1 ball Pizza Dough (page 60)

Semolina flour for sprinkling

½ cup Cooked Red Sauce (page 66), or as needed

¾ cup shredded low-moisture mozzarella

2 tablespoons thinly sliced caperberries

Extra-virgin olive oil for drizzling

1 pinch kosher salt

Freshly grated Parmigiano-Reggiano for finishing

Red pepper flakes for finishing

1 One hour before you plan to make the pizza, place your pizza stone on the bottom rack of your oven and preheat to 550°F (or, if the oven won't get that hot, as hot as it will go). This will superheat the pizza stone.

2 Shape the dough as instructed in steps 9 and 10 on page 62.

3 Using both hands, transfer the dough to the prepared pizza peel. If the dough gets misshapen during the transfer, nudge it back into the shape of a circle. Grab the peel by the handle and flick your wrist to shake it back and forth a bit, to ensure the dough isn't stuck to the peel.

4 Using a ladle, spoon the sauce into the center of the dough and then spiral it out toward the edges with the back of the ladle, leaving a ½-inch rim around the edge. Distribute the mozz and caperberries evenly over the sauce, then drizzle a bit of olive oil over everything.

5 Working quickly to maintain the oven's temperature, transfer the pizza from the peel to the stone. To do this, angle the pizza peel at about 45 degrees with the edge touching the back of the stone. The pizza should slide off the peel and make contact with the back of the stone. Swiftly pull away the peel and the pizza should land in a tidy circle on the stone.

6 Cook for 3½ minutes, then, using the peel, rotate the pizza 180 degrees to ensure even cooking and cook for 2½ minutes more. The cheese should be melted and there should be flecks of char on the crust.

7 Using the peel, remove the pie from the oven. Drizzle a bit more olive oil over the pizza, then finish with the salt, some Parm, and red pepper flakes. Serve immediately.

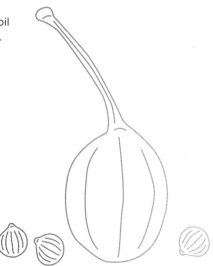

PAPA PICANTE
(SOPRESSATA AND HOT HONEY)

MAKES ONE 12- TO 14-INCH PIZZA

One of my favorite flavor combos in the world is spicy fatty meat with some sweet heat. It's the underlying concept of so many of my favorite dishes: Thai curries with wild intense chiles, palm sugar, and glistening meat; Kansas City barbecue with molasses-y sauce and a hit of cayenne. Each bite of this spectacular circular-experience pizza explodes with flavor: sweet, spicy, salty. You can buy hot honey at most grocery stores, or make your own if you wanna get fancy and customize your heat level (see Note).

1 ball Pizza Dough (page 60)

Semolina flour for sprinkling

½ cup Cooked Red Sauce (page 66), or as needed

¾ cup shredded low-moisture mozzarella

1½ to 2 ounces sopressata, sliced as thin as possible (about 15 slices)

Thinly sliced pickled serrano or Fresno chiles (see page 69) for topping

Hot honey for drizzling

Freshly grated Parmigiano-Reggiano for finishing

1 One hour before you plan to make the pizza, place your pizza stone on the bottom rack of your oven and preheat to 550°F (or, if the oven won't get that hot, as hot as it will go). This will superheat the pizza stone.

2 Shape the dough as instructed in steps 9 and 10 on page 62.

3 Using both hands, transfer the dough to the prepared pizza peel. If the dough gets misshapen during the transfer, nudge it back into the shape of a circle. Grab the peel by the handle and flick your wrist to shake it back and forth a bit, to ensure the dough isn't stuck to the peel.

4 Using a ladle, spoon the sauce into the center of the dough and then spiral it out toward the edges with the back of the ladle, leaving a ½-inch rim around the edge. Distribute three-fourths of the mozz evenly over the sauce, then evenly distribute the sopressata and pickled chiles over the top. Sprinkle with the remaining mozz.

5 Working quickly to maintain the oven's temperature, transfer the pizza from the peel to the stone. To do this, angle the pizza peel at about 45 degrees with the edge touching the back of the stone. The pizza should slide off the peel and make contact with the back of the stone. Swiftly pull away the peel and the pizza should land in a tidy circle on the stone.

6 Cook for 3½ minutes, then, using the peel, rotate the pizza 180 degrees to ensure even cooking and cook for 2½ minutes more. The cheese should be melted and there should be flecks of char on the crust.

7 Using the peel, remove the pie from the oven. Drizzle the hot honey over the pizza, then finish with some Parm. Serve immediately.

Note: To make hot honey, in a small saucepan, combine 1 cup honey with a couple (maybe two or three or four, depending on how spicy you're feeling) sliced fresh chiles. Bring to a simmer and cook over the lowest heat setting for 1 hour, or until you reach the spice level you prefer. At that point you should strain out the chiles. You can store the honey for a few months in the fridge.

ROASTED MUSHROOM, FONTINA, FRIED SAGE, AND CRISPY SPECK

MAKES ONE 12- TO 14-INCH PIZZA

½ cup extra-virgin olive oil, plus more for drizzling

2 pieces speck

5 sage leaves

1 ball Pizza Dough (page 60)

Semolina flour for sprinkling

⅓ cup Pepper Cream (page 67), or as needed

⅓ cup shredded low-moisture mozzarella

¼ cup shredded fontina

¼ cup Roasted Mushrooms (facing page)

Freshly grated Pecorino Romano for finishing

The amount of ingredients on this pizza is PUSHING it for me. I would never order a supreme pizza. It's just too much! But this is a classic combo and it just works. When you get a bite of fontina, mushroom, speck (a lightly smoked style of ham that hails from northeast Italy—you can sub prosciutto if you can't find it), and sage at the same time, you are in ZAH HEAVEN.

1. One hour before you plan to make the pizza, place your pizza stone on the bottom rack of your oven and preheat to 550°F (or, if the oven won't get that hot, as hot as it will go). This will superheat the pizza stone. Line a plate with a double layer of paper towels.

2. In a medium saucepan over medium-high heat, warm the ½ cup olive oil. Once it's hot and shimmering, add the speck and cook until brittle and browned, about 30 seconds, then transfer to the prepared plate to cool. Break the speck into large shards. Add the sage to the oil; it will bubble up, then once it dies down, the sage should be crispy and fragrant. Transfer to the plate with the speck.

3. Shape the dough as instructed in steps 9 and 10 on page 62.

4. Using both hands, transfer the dough to the prepared pizza peel. If the dough gets misshapen during the transfer, nudge it back into the shape of a circle. Grab the peel by the handle and flick your wrist to shake it back and forth a bit, to ensure the dough isn't stuck to the peel.

5. Using a ladle, spoon the cream into the center of the dough and then spiral it out toward the edges with the back of the ladle, leaving a ½-inch rim around the edge. Distribute half the mozz and fontina, all the mushrooms, and then the remaining mozz and fontina evenly over the cream. Arrange the sage leaves and torn speck neatly on top.

6. Working quickly to maintain the oven's temperature, transfer the pizza from the peel to the stone. To do this, angle the pizza peel at about 45 degrees with the edge touching the back of the stone. The pizza should slide off the peel and make contact with the back of the stone. Swiftly pull away the peel and the pizza should land in a tidy circle on the stone.

7. Cook for 3½ minutes, then, using the peel, rotate the pizza 180 degrees to ensure even cooking and cook for 2½ minutes more. The cheese should be melted and there should be flecks of char on the crust.

8. Using the peel, remove the pie from the oven. Drizzle with olive oil, then finish with some Pecorino. Serve immediately.

1 Preheat your oven to 400°F.

2 In a medium bowl, toss the mushrooms and rosemary in the olive oil, then transfer to a baking sheet. Season with salt, then roast until browned, 10 to 15 minutes. Store airtight in the fridge for up to 5 days.

ROASTED MUSHROOMS

MAKES ABOUT ½ CUP

2½ cups sliced cremini mushrooms

¼ teaspoon chopped fresh rosemary

2 tablespoons extra-virgin olive oil

Kosher salt

ANCHOVY AND LEMON

MAKES ONE 12- TO 14-INCH PIZZA

1 ball Pizza Dough (page 60)

Semolina flour for sprinkling

⅓ cup Pepper Cream
(page 67), or as needed

⅓ cup shredded
low-moisture mozzarella

1 lemon, sliced as thinly
as possible and seeded

1 pinch kosher salt

8 anchovy fillets (such as
Ortiz brand)

Extra-virgin olive oil
for drizzling

Chopped fresh parsley
for sprinkling

Freshly ground black pepper

When in Naples, you *have* to go to Pizzeria da Attilio. I can honestly say it is one of the most insane pizza experiences of my life. Not only are the pizzas perfect but the people who run the place are so warm and loving and inspirational.

My first time there, I went nuts and ordered *sooo* many pizzas: classic marinara, zucchini flowers with tomatoes and crushed pistachios, and a pancetta-and-mushroom star-shaped pizza with a ricotta-filled crust. But the pizza that totally blew my mind, and that I just had to try to re-create at home, was a simple white pie with paper-thin slices of lemon and big, beautiful fresh anchovies.

Outside of Italy, I'll probably never find anchovies as perfect as the ones they serve at Attilio, but it's worth going to an Italian grocer or specialty shop and asking for the best anchovies they have. It's important that you choose a nice, thin-skinned lemon and wash it well. Look for a smooth one rather than the big boy with a craggy surface (those tend to have a thick, bitter pith).

1 One hour before you plan to make the pizza, place your pizza stone on the bottom rack of your oven and preheat to 550°F (or, if the oven won't get that hot, as hot as it will go). This will superheat the pizza stone.

2 Shape the dough as instructed in steps 9 and 10 on page 62.

3 Using both hands, transfer the dough to the prepared pizza peel. If the dough gets misshapen during the transfer, nudge it back into the shape of a circle. Grab the peel by the handle and flick your wrist to shake it back and forth a bit, to ensure the dough isn't stuck to the peel.

4 Using a ladle, spoon the cream into the center of the dough and then spiral it out toward the edges with the back of the ladle, leaving a ½-inch rim around the edge. Distribute half of the mozz evenly over the cream. Place the lemon slices evenly over the cheese without overlapping them (figure about ten slices), then sprinkle the salt over the lemons and top with the remaining mozz.

5 Working quickly to maintain the oven's temperature, transfer the pizza from the peel to the stone. To do this, angle the pizza peel at about 45 degrees with the edge touching the back of the stone. The pizza should slide off the peel and make contact with the back of the stone. Swiftly pull away the peel and the pizza should land in a tidy circle on the stone.

6 Cook for 3½ minutes, then, using the peel, rotate the pizza 180 degrees to ensure even cooking and cook for 2½ minutes more. The cheese should be melted and there should be flecks of char on the crust.

7 Using the peel, remove the pie from the oven. Arrange the anchovies attractively on top of the pizza, drizzle with some olive oil, and then sprinkle with parsley and black pepper. Serve immediately.

CHEESY DIPPERS

MAKES ONE 10-INCH PIZZA

I love a pan pie and I LOVE to dip. So here's an homage to the pan pizzas of my youth, made with a beautifully fermented homemade dough and high-quality mozz. It's one part Pequod's, one part Papa John's breadsticks.

1 Position a rack in the center of your oven and preheat to 550°F (or, if the oven won't get that hot, as hot as it will go). Ten minutes before you plan to bake the pizza, place a 12-inch cast-iron skillet in the oven to superheat it.

2 Meanwhile, in a small bowl, combine the butter and garlic and stir to incorporate.

3 Shape the dough, as instructed in steps 9 and 10 on page 62, into a 10-inch disk so that it will fit snugly into the bottom of your skillet. (This pizza will be a little thicker than usual.)

4 Using an oven mitt, remove the skillet from the oven. It's gonna be real hot. Add the olive oil to the skillet—it should sizzle.

5 Add the dough to the skillet, then, using a pastry brush, spread the garlic-butter evenly over the entire surface. Distribute the mozz over the top, all the way to the edges of the crust. Push some mozz into the edges of where the dough meets the pan. (This is how you get that gorgeous cheese lace.) Sprinkle the Parm over everything.

6 Once again using the oven mitt, return the skillet to the oven and cook until the cheese is golden brown and bubbly, about 8 minutes.

7 Using a spatula and tongs (if needed), transfer the pizza to a cutting board and sprinkle with sea salt. Cut the pie in half and then cut each half (perpendicular to where you just cut) into 1-inch strips. Transfer to a serving plate and serve with the sauce on the side for dipping.

3 tablespoons melted unsalted butter

2 garlic cloves, finely minced

1 ball Pizza Dough (page 60)

2 tablespoons extra-virgin olive oil

1¼ cups shredded low-moisture mozzarella

1 tablespoon freshly grated Parmigiano-Reggiano

Flaky sea salt (such as Maldon)

1½ cups Fresh Red Sauce (page 66), at room temperature

PERSONAL PAN PEP PEP

MAKES FOUR 6-INCH PAN PIZZAS

Personal Pizza Dough

325 grams / 1⅜ cups 70°F filtered water

500 grams / 3½ cups bread flour

25 grams / 2 tablespoons extra-virgin olive oil

15 grams / 3½ teaspoons packed brown sugar

1 gram / ⅓ teaspoon instant dried yeast

10 grams / 1 tablespoon kosher salt

1 cup Fresh Red Sauce (page 66)

1¾ cups shredded low-moisture mozzarella

Kosher salt

Extra-virgin olive oil for drizzling

2 ounces sliced pepperoni

Freshly grated Parmigiano-Reggiano for sprinkling

When I started writing this book, I knew I had to try to reverse-engineer the Pizza Hut pan pie at home, but ramp it up big time, using legit ingredients and techniques. At the time, Pizza Lord Noel Brohner was developing a pan-style pizza for a fast-casual restaurant in LA and texted me some of his test bakes. I freaked out because they looked so damn delicious, and I ended up driving across town to watch him in action and take some notes.

For once, I'm gonna tell you it's okay to use grocery store pepperoni. I'll allow it just this one time because it is so flavorful and oily, true to the spirit of Pizza Hut. If you would like to mix the dough by hand, see the variation on page 63. This is a double-bake process, but it's easy and so worth the effort.

1 To make the dough: In the bowl of a stand mixer fitted with the dough hook attachment, add the water and then the flour, olive oil, and brown sugar. Mix at the lowest speed setting for 3½ minutes, scraping down the sides of the bowl as necessary, until the ingredients are well incorporated. Turn off the mixer and let the dough rest for 20 minutes.

2 Add the yeast to the mixture and mix for 1 minute at the lowest speed setting, then add the salt and mix for 1 minute more. Turn the speed to the next setting and mix for an additional 4 minutes. Do the "windowpane test" to check the dough's gluten development: Pull a small piece of dough and stretch it up between your fingers. You should be able to stretch it so that it becomes translucent (like a windowpane) with threads of gluten visible without the dough ripping. If it rips, mix for another minute or two to develop the gluten further.

3 Lightly oil a plastic dough bin or large bowl and gently transfer the dough into it, using a plastic dough scraper to assist. Cover with the lid or plastic wrap and allow to rest for 30 minutes.

4 Time for the first stretch and fold! Lightly oil your hands, then grab about a third of the dough mass, pull it up and away, and fold it over the top of the dough. Spin the tub or bowl 180 degrees and repeat the process. Repeat twice more for four total folds, so your dough looks like a nice li'l package. Flip the whole mass of dough upside down so the exposed top is smooth and round.

5 Cover the dough and let rest for another 30 minutes. Then repeat the whole "stretch and fold" process again. Now re-cover the dough and place the whole thing in the refrigerator overnight to ferment and develop flavor. Just like Heimy, this dough needs at least 8 hours of beauty sleep.

6 The next day, remove the dough from the refrigerator 4 hours before you plan to bake the pizzas and allow to rest, covered, at room temperature for 30 minutes. Generously oil the bottom and sides of four 6-inch, straight-edged cake pans.

continued

7 Tip the dough out onto a clean, floured work surface. Cut the dough into four 170-gram portions. (You should have a bit of dough left over at the end, which you can either discard or bake later for a little snack.)

8 Flour your hands and grab a piece of dough. Knock off any excess flour from the bottom. Begin to fold the sides underneath the dough mass, pinching the seams closed at the bottom as you go. You're sort of stretching and creating surface tension on the dough by pulling the top and tucking it under. It's a little tricky at first but you'll get the hang of it. The goal is to create a smooth uniform ball with a tightly closed seam underneath. Place each shaped ball into the prepared cake pans. Cover the cake pans with plastic wrap. Let the balls rest until they're about one and a half times their original size, about 3½ hours.

9 When you're ready to make the pizzas, place your pizza stone on the bottom rack of your oven and preheat to 550°F (or, if the oven won't get that hot, as hot as it will go).

10 Using your fingertips, dimple the dough and spread it out so it fills the pan. Add 1 tablespoon sauce followed by 1½ tablespoons mozz to each pie.

11 Bake #1—This gets your foundation. To parcook the pizzas, place the pans directly on the pizza stone and bake for 7 minutes—this will help you get an extra-crispy bottom. Remove the pans from the oven.

12 Top each pizza with an additional 3 tablespoons sauce and 5 tablespoons mozz, making sure to go all the way to the edge of the pan and a li'l under the dough. Those bits are gonna form that super-crispy cheese lace. Sprinkle each pizza with a small pinch of salt and drizzle with olive oil, then top with the pepperoni, overlapping each piece a bit to cover the surface. Finally, sprinkle a teensy bit more mozz over the 'roni.

13 Bake #2—Place the pans back in the oven, this time on the middle rack instead of on the pizza stone (you don't want the bottom to burn, and you want to make sure the interior stays soft and pillowy). Bake until the toppings are beautifully melty and crispy, another 5½ to 6½ minutes.

14 Pull your pep peps from the oven, lift out of the pans with a spatula, and sprinkle with a bit of Parm. Serve immediately.

Note: Look for 6-inch nonstick cake pans at kitchenware stores or online. (Make sure to buy a *cake* pan—not a pie pan—that has straight, rather than tapered, 2-inch sides. And nonstick is essential; anything else and you will have to season it before baking, which is kind of a pain.)

PIZZA PARTY

There is no better party than the pizza party. Cheese, wine, friends—what more do you need? But to ensure your pizza party is a happy fun-times zone for even you, the chef, you'll want to do a little bit of pizza prep.

The key is to set up all your topping stations ahead of time so you can get an assembly line going once you start putting pizzas in the oven. This preparation is called mise en place. Anthony Bourdain

summed up the importance of the "mise" in *Kitchen Confidential: "Mise en place* is the religion of all good line cooks. . . . The universe is in order when your station is set up the way you like it; you know where to find everything with your eyes closed, everything you need during the course of the shift is at the ready at arm's reach, your defenses are deployed."

Your pizza station will be beautiful if you set it up properly. It may even inspire you to create new pies on the fly when you can see all your ingredients laid out. So put everything in easily accessible bowls close to where you're going to dress the pie. Give your ingredients time to come to room temp before you start dressing the pizzas. You wanna move quickly once you shape your pie and place it on the peel, so don't put the cheese in one place and the sauce somewhere else on the other side of the kitchen. Most important of all: Make sure you appoint a deputy to refill your wine while you are baking. You will be in the ZONE and FOCUSED and need WINE FUEL.

After you bang out a few perfect pies, let your friends give it a go. Have them design their own signature pies. Like I said before, it's an amazing feeling to pull a freshly baked pizza that YOU MADE with your own hands. Your friends will love it.

PIZZA WINES

Pie and vino is a no-brainer. I personally start with some grower champagne (see page 238) or a crisp pét-nat to get my taste buds activated. Then move to light reds or more sparkling wine—the bubbles and acidity cut through the fat of the pizza amazingly well. One of my all-time favorite pairings is pizza and Lambrusco, a sparkling red wine from Emilia-Romagna that I drank pretty much every day when we were filming *Master of None* in Modena.

Lambrusco can sometimes be hard to shop for, so go to your local wine store and ask the staff to help you pick out something good. There are a few Lambrusco makers in Emilia-Romagna who are taking the time to really do it right. Their wines have deep cherry notes, soft effervescence, and a subtle funkiness that I just can't get enough of. Make sure to serve this chilled, like you would for any other sparkling wine.

Some great pizza wines

Etna Rosso (Sicily): Volcanic red from Mount Etna. Try producers such as Benanti or Tenuta delle Terre Nerre.

Lambrusco (Emilia-Romagna): Look for natural producers such as Camillo Donati, Saetti, and Vittorio Graziano.

Las Jaras Glou Glou (California): This is a shameless plug, but dude, it's a perfect pizza wine. Light, juicy red made from a rotating blend of grapes such as Zinfandel, Carignan, and Petite Sirah.

When I think about Grandma Foods, I think about

my literal grandmas—especially my mom's mom, my oma, who lived in Germany and worked magic with humble ingredients, like stew meat, potatoes, and cabbage. She and my opa never had a lot of money, so for them, being frugal in the kitchen was a necessity. That's why they always had an edible garden and would pickle vegetables in the spring to last them throughout the entire year.

My heritage is German, but once I was able to travel a bit, I realized that Grandma Foods are truly universal. In every culture, you'll find a home cooking tradition of taking affordable, abundant regional ingredients—staples such as potatoes, tomatoes, rice, or onions—and cooking them with time and care to create something exquisite.

There is no more comforting memory than walking into Grandma's house on a Sunday. She gives you that big grandma hug and then you start sniffin' that meat that has been slowly roasting in the oven for hours. Then it's time to hit the candy in the crystal candy dish, making sure to save enough room for mashed taters and the cake that's coming later!

Something to remember is that most grandmas are wise as fuck. They've been through far more than you, so sit down and listen to them. Take their advice on relationships and, of course, how to braise a brisket.

To me, the food that perfectly epitomizes the concept of Grandma Foods is pasta. Pasta is as important to me as water and air. It's another of those visceral comfort foods that transport me to a happy place in my childhood. It's also one of the most satisfying dishes you can make at home. A bowl of pasta is unpretentious and doesn't require expensive ingredients. Grab my hand and I'll teach you a few recipes that will up your game and take you to Pasta Paradise.

I've been a pasta connoisseur my whole life, but it wasn't until I traveled to Italy that I started to understand the true art behind the dish. It's about simplicity. It's about cooking the pasta just right. It's about respecting the ingredients and using them in the correct ratios to deliver a balanced bite.

On one of my more intense culinary expeditions through Italy, Aziz and I traveled up and down the country in search of the most premium bites, as well as a location for Season 2 of *Master of None*. We needed a place with character, not too many tourists, and, most important of all, PASTA.

We started in Rome, where my friend Katie Parla, a brilliant culinary historian and writer, took us on a whirlwind food tour that included the restaurant Roscioli. There, we ate some of the best amatriciana and carbonara of my life, drank beautiful Italian wines, and, fueled by the spirit of the ancients, danced around Roman ruins for hours. We were possessed by that crispy guanciale! There is video evidence of this special food dance choreographed to a Kanye song somewhere online.

From Rome, we traveled through Tuscany, Puglia, Sicily, and then back up to Modena. That's where we struck gold! Modena is an ancient city and the central hub of Emilia-Romagna, which is one of the most legendary food regions in the world. Parmigiano-Reggiano. Balsamic vinegar. Prosciutto di Parma, mortadella, Lambrusco. These are just a few of the world-famous products that hail from Emilia-Romagna. It was perfect for us.

At the end of each day of shooting, we'd pick out a new regional restaurant to try. Some of our favorites even made it into the show. One evening, after we had wrapped shooting at a restaurant, Hosteria Giusti—this tiny place with only four tables, where I had eaten one of the best meals of my life—Aziz and I were having a drink at one of the bars off the piazza when Massimo Bottura, the chef of Osteria Francescana, walked in. He came right over to us and sternly asked, "Why aren't you shooting at my restaurant?"

We laughed and were, like, "Dude, you're the number-one restaurant in the world; we don't want to bother you!" But he wouldn't have it. "No. I am part of this town. You guys come in for lunch tomorrow. We'll shoot with real food, we'll shoot with real wine."

The next day, we just kept the cameras rolling as the meal unfolded in the private dining room at Osteria Francescana. That is why, if you've seen this scene, it looks like our minds are being totally freaking blown by the food we're eating—those are *very* real reactions you are seeing. In between takes, we passed bites to our crew, so they could try this insanely delicious food. BONK!

In wine, we talk a lot about *terroir*—in a literal sense, the way land and soil influence grapes, but more poetically, the way a region's landscape and culture and history shape its wine. I feel as though I really learned to appreciate terroir by tasting pasta across Italy. You can drive from Venice to Sicily in a day, yet taste a hundred distinct regional pastas along the way. There are the subtle cuttlefish pastas of Venice; Tuscan pastas with assertive, gamey boar sauce; classic Roman pastas, like cacio e pepe and carbonara; and vibrant, vegetal pastas in Sicily with pesto made from sanapo, a variety of local green.

The pasta recipes that follow may seem simple on the surface, but they require finesse. Salt your pasta water. Don't over-Parm. Talk to your cheesemonger and buy the nice chunk of aged, red cow Parm. (Notice how your taste buds tingle when you get a bite of that umami-rich cheese dust.) Get a nice bottle of finishing olive oil—it'll be different than the olive oil you use for cooking. A light, lemony finishing oil can completely elevate a dish. Pasta is something that I hold sacred. Italians have been perfecting these recipes for 1,000-plus years. So, when you're just learning to make it, start with the classics, then go off on your own path.

PASTAS THAT HAVE MOVED ME

1. **Macaroni with duck ragù:** Hosteria Giusti, Modena, Italy

2. **Spaghetti with sanapo (local spinach):** Ristorante Crocifisso, Noto (Sicily), Italy

3. **La Matriciana o Amatriciana (rigatoni amatriciana):** Roscioli Ristorante, Rome, Italy

4. **Spaghetti with Formentera shrimp:** Ristorante Can Carlos, Formentera, Spain

5. **Pici with wild boar ragù and bread crumbs:** Antica Osteria Da Divo, Siena, Italy

6. **Cacio e pepe with uni:** Wildair, New York City

7. **Tortellini in Parmigiano-Reggiano cream:** Osteria Francescana, Modena, Italy

8. **Tagliolini cacio e pepe:** Ristorante Roma Sparita, Rome, Italy

9. **100-layer lasagna:** Del Posto, New York City

10. **Spaghetti vongole (spaghetti with clams):** Da Adolfo, Positano, Italy

BIG BUD

LI'L BUD

FRESH EGG PASTA

MAKES ABOUT 1½ POUNDS (4 TO 6 SERVINGS)

Every now and then there's a perfect moment when my TV career and my food obsession intersect and true magic happens. One of my favorites was when we were filming a scene for *Master of None*, where Dev learns how to roll out pasta by hand with a mattarello, which is a specialized wooden pasta rolling pin, from an Italian nonna. The amazing part is that he and I actually got to learn how to do it to shoot the scene. So basically I got to learn how to make pasta from the best of the best and call it "work."

Madi and I recently acquired a mattarello from LA Pasta King Evan Funke's guy in Bologna. We love and cherish this perfect tool. It takes a li'l extra time and effort to roll out the sheets by hand, but it feels so beautiful and authentic. The click-clacking of the mattarello hitting the table when you lift and spin your dough takes me back to those special moments in Modena. A pasta machine certainly makes things easier—so I use that method here and give hand-rolling instructions as a variation. You can buy a standalone machine; or if you already have a KitchenAid stand mixer, I recommend their pasta attachment.

3 cups all-purpose flour

4 eggs

4 teaspoons kosher salt

4 teaspoons extra-virgin olive oil

Semolina flour for dusting

1 On a clean countertop or work surface, mound 2½ cups of the all-purpose flour in a large pile. Form a well in the middle so that your flour looks like a volcano. Make sure the well is wide enough to hold all the eggs without them spilling over the edges of the crater!

2 Crack the eggs into the crater of the volcano. Add the salt and olive oil and, using a fork, beat the eggs. At this stage, a bit of the flour will work its way into the liquid in the well. Your dough is starting to come together.

3 Continue gently beating the ingredients with the fork, pulling in more flour a bit at a time, until the flour is moistened and the mixture turns into a lumpy paste. At this point, you can ditch the fork. Flour your hands and use them to incorporate all the flour into the wet ingredients. Start kneading the dough by folding the raggedy mound over itself, pushing the dough against your work surface, turning it over, and folding it again. If the dough seems too wet and won't come together, add in a bit of your reserved flour. The longer you work the dough, the more it will stiffen up and become less sticky. You may not even use all of the flour you started with—every dough is different.

4 Continue to knead the dough by hand for 10 minutes—this is hard work. A true friend will feed you sips of wine as you're kneading, to keep your spirits high. Lean into the dough with your full weight, pressing with your palms to work the dough against the work surface. You'll know the dough is done when it is smooth and shiny on the outside.

continued

5 Shape the dough into a ball and wrap it tightly in plastic wrap, then refrigerate for at least 1 hour or up to 1 day. This resting period allows the dough to relax a bit so that your pasta is tender.

6 When it's time to roll out your dough, generously dust a baking sheet with semolina (this is where you'll store the cut pasta). Remove the dough from the fridge and cut it into fourths.

7 Working with one piece at a time (keep the remaining dough wrapped in plastic to keep it from drying out), form the dough ball into a roughly even rectangle. Set your pasta machine to its widest setting, then feed the dough in by its short side and roll it through. Fold the dough piece in half or thirds so that the raw edge is roughly the width of your machine. Now feed the dough through the machine again—still on its widest setting— leading with the raw (not folded) edge. Repeat this one more time—you're basically giving the dough an extra mini-knead. At this point, if the surface of the dough still doesn't look smooth and homogenous, keep rolling it through the machine (without folding it, though) at the widest setting until it does.

8 Once the surface of the dough looks smooth, change the level of the machine to the next setting, then roll the dough through. Repeat this process and keep rolling the dough through, one setting at a time. Once you get to the narrower settings, you'll need to lightly dust both sides of the dough with semolina so it doesn't stick to itself. You also might find that the pasta sheet gets long and unwieldy; you can either cut it to a more manageable length, or call on a buddy to help you—one person feeds the dough through the machine while the other person cranks and catches it out of the other end.

9 Roll the dough until it is very thin (UNLESS you are planning to make garganelli, see page 106; in that case, roll it a bit thicker, about 1 millimeter)—you should be able to see the outline of your hand through it, but it shouldn't be totally see-though. This is usually the last or second-to-last setting on your pasta machine.

10 If you're making pappardelle or tagliatelle (see page 106), allow the sheets of pasta to dry out until they're flexible and don't crack when you roll them into a cylinder, but not so wet that they're sticky and the sheets stick together, about 10 minutes. (If you're making garganelli, skip this rest period and immediately cut the sheets into squares.)

11 If you're not cooking the pasta immediately, gather it into small bundles and store it, uncovered, at room temperature until completely dried out, up to 24 hours. At this stage, you can store it in a box as you would store-bought dried pasta—keep it in a cool pantry for a week or two. (This only works if you've thoroughly dried the pasta, though—any moisture might develop into mold and spoil it.)

12 When ready to cook, bring a large pot of salted water to a boil. Add the pasta, stir once to ensure it doesn't stick to the bottom of the pot, and cook until it's tender (you don't want to cook fresh pasta until al dente). Timing will depend on how fresh versus dried your pasta is; it's ready when it floats to the top of the water. Super-fresh pasta can take as little as 2 minutes, so taste-test strands until the pieces are tender but not mushy—they should still have a bit of snap.

Variation

To roll the dough by hand, lightly flour a clean countertop or work surface as well as your rolling implement, which can be a rolling pin, mattarello, or, in a pinch, wine bottle. Press the dough flat with the palm of your hands. Using the pin and working from the center outward, roll the dough into a circle. Every couple of passes, flip the dough over and sprinkle a bit more flour on your work surface, so it doesn't stick. After rolling, proceed as directed to cut the pasta dough as desired.

continued

FRESH EGG PASTA, CONTINUED

Pasta Shapes

Garganelli: To make this shape, you'll need a piece of special equipment. A garganelli/gnocchi board is a rectangular piece of wood with grooves in it. It is inexpensive and easy to find in kitchenware stores and online (try Fante's Kitchen Shop at fantes.com). If you want to get super-traditional, you can try to track down an authentic Italian pettine (which translates to "comb")— it looks kind of like a mini loom. You'll also need a smooth, wooden dowel with a ¼-inch diameter (typically this comes with the garganelli board).

Cut the sheets of pasta into 2-inch squares, then let the squares rest for 10 minutes to dry out just slightly. Lay the garganelli board lengthwise in front of you so that the groove lines are oriented vertically. Lay a pasta square diagonally on the board so that it's oriented like a diamond, with one tip facing up. Place the wooden dowel on the bottom tip of the pasta diamond, then nudge that tip around the dowel with your fingers. Roll the dowel up the diamond with steady but gentle pressure so that the pasta curls up around it. This will most likely take a few tries to get right, but eventually you'll end up with a ridged tube shape. Slip the garganelli off the dowel and onto the semolina-dusted baking sheet and continue with the remaining squares of dough.

Pappardelle: Cut the sheets of pasta into strips that are 8 inches long and 1 inch wide. (If you want to get fancy, use a fluted pastry wheel, which gives you nice crinkly edges.) Store the finished pasta on the semolina-dusted baking sheet until ready to cook.

Tagliatelle: Sprinkle each sheet of pasta with semolina to avoid sticking, then roll each sheet lengthwise into a loose cylinder about 3 inches wide. Cut the cylinder perpendicular to its rolled edge into strips about ¼ inch wide, so that when you unroll them you get long, ¼-inch-wide ribbons.

Picking the Right Pasta Shape

Pasta is a device that is designed to get sauce in your mouth. When you think of it in those terms, you start to understand why certain shapes are traditionally paired with certain sauces. You wouldn't want to serve a chunky boar ragù with thin, delicate spaghettini—the pieces of meat would slide right off the pasta. Pappardelle, by contrast, is wider and has enough surface area to scoop up larger pieces of meat. Tagliatelle, one of the classic shapes of Bologna, is a bit narrower than pappardelle, which makes it a great vehicle for the ground-meat sauce that is ragù Bolognese.

But back to that spaghettini. There's a reason why classic Roman dishes such as cacio e pepe and carbonara are traditionally made with tonnarelli and spaghetti, respectively. Those are silky, emulsified sauces that want to cling to each strand of pasta. A thinner pasta shape helps you really appreciate the subtlety of the sauce.

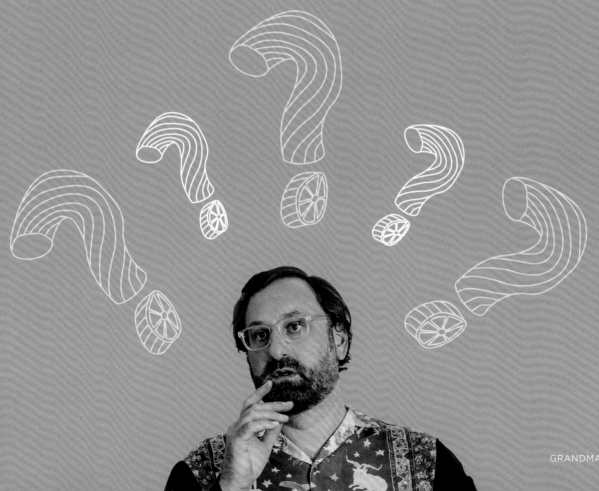

NONNA SAUCE

MAKES ABOUT 4½ CUPS

Sundays in the Heimy household are all about garlic and tomatoes. I put on my apron, crank the Italo disco, and get to work making this classic sauce. Soon, incredible aromas fill the entire house, and I feel like I'm back in South Philly, where you can sometimes smell the gorgeous nonna cookin' from the street.

The most important step is to make sure to talk to your sauce. Stir it tenderly and tell it that you love it. This sauce is your baby, so make sure to simmer it low and slow, over very gentle heat.

This recipe makes more than enough sauce for a big pot of spaghetti or a batch of Chicken Parm (page 153), so store any leftovers airtight in your freezer for up to 2 months. To reheat, let the sauce thaw at room temp and then warm it in a saucepan over low heat. While you're at it, you can even double the recipe so you have extra for whenever the nonna craving comes calling.

½ cup extra-virgin olive oil

8 garlic cloves, thinly sliced

6 large basil leaves

1 medium yellow onion, finely diced

Two 28-ounce cans whole peeled tomatoes

1 teaspoon dried oregano

1 teaspoon red pepper flakes

Kosher salt

1 In a Dutch oven or a large stockpot over very low heat, warm the olive oil, then add the garlic and two of the basil leaves. Sauté gently, stirring occasionally, until the garlic is lightly golden, about 10 minutes. Watch the pot carefully and remove the garlic and basil as soon as the garlic is golden. (If you burn the garlic, dump it and start over, because burned garlic will make the sauce bitter.) Set aside the sautéed garlic and basil.

2 Turn the heat to medium, add the onion to the garlicky oil and sauté until soft and translucent, about 5 minutes.

3 Add the tomatoes, oregano, red pepper flakes, 1½ teaspoons salt, and reserved garlic and basil to the pot and stir to combine. Using the back of a spoon, start crushing the tomatoes into smaller pieces.

4 Lower the heat so the pot just barely simmers and cook for 1 hour, stirring every so often and pressing the tomatoes with the back of your spoon so that they fall apart and dissolve into the sauce. DON'T FORGET TO TELL YOUR SAUCE THAT YOU LOVE IT. Maybe sing a song to encourage it. The sauce is done when the tomatoes have really melted into it and everything smells amazing. If you ain't into the chunky vibes, you can use a potato masher or an immersion blender to break down the sauce a li'l more—it's up to you. Season with salt, if needed, before serving.

CACIO E PEPE
IN PARM BOWLS

MAKES 2 SERVINGS

½ pound dried bucatini pasta

1½ tablespoons unsalted butter

1 teaspoon whole black peppercorns, crushed (see Heimy's Hint, page 14)

1 cup freshly grated Parmigiano-Reggiano

¾ cup freshly grated Pecorino Romano

Parm Bowls (page 115) for serving

Freshly ground black pepper

This deep, dank, creamy pasta is the first thing I crave when I arrive in Rome. So, after I land, I make a beeline for Roma Sparita, which is where I first encountered this EYOB (eat your own bowl) preparation. Along with spaghetti carbonara, cacio e pepe is one of the most iconic Roman-style pasta dishes there is, and it's a recipe you should learn by heart. It translates to "Pecorino and pepper," and that's really all it is—so you should always have the necessary ingredients in your pantry. Make sure to use fresh peppercorns here (if yours are on the staler side, you might have to use more than what's called for) and crush them yourself (don't buy preground stuff). Definitely grate the finest Parm and Pecorino you can get your hands on. Does this already insanely rich dish NEED a Parm bowl? Of course not, but trust me, you need to try it. This is Heimy Style at its peak.

❶ Bring a large pot of salted water to a boil. Add the pasta, cook according to the package instructions, and then drain; reserving a couple cups of the starchy pasta water.

❷ In a large saucepan over medium-high heat, melt the butter, then add the crushed peppercorns and cook until toasty and fragrant but not burned, about 90 seconds. Add ½ cup of the reserved pasta water and simmer for 1 minute. Turn the heat to medium, then add the pasta and the Parm. Using tongs, stir to integrate the pasta, about 1 minute. At this point you should have a loose, liquidy sauce that is shiny and coats every strand of pasta.

❸ Remove the pan from the heat, add the Pecorino, and stir again to combine. The sauce should be rich and creamy, but you can add more pasta water if needed to reach the right consistency.

❹ Place a Parm bowl on each serving plate, then divide the pasta evenly among the bowls and finish with a pinch of freshly ground pepper. Serve immediately.

continued

1 Preheat your oven to 350°F. Line a baking sheet with parchment paper.

2 Place ¾ cup of the Parm onto the parchment and form into a circle. The cheese should be spread evenly and thinly—but not so thin that there are holes where you can see through to the parchment.

3 Bake the Parm until bubbly and browned a bit, about 7 minutes. Remove from the oven, then grab a bowl (a standard cereal bowl works best) and place the bowl, right-side up, on the center of the cheese circle. Using oven mitts or a kitchen towel, flip the bowl plus the cheese and parchment so the bowl is upside down. Press and drape the cheese and parchment so it molds around the bowl. Peel off the parchment and let the cheese harden over the bowl for 5 minutes.

4 Meanwhile, repeat with the remaining ¾ cup cheese to form a second bowl and then serve.

PARM BOWLS

MAKES 2 BOWLS

1½ cups freshly grated
Parmigiano-Reggiano

EMILIO'S POMODORO

MAKES 4 SERVINGS

This recipe is proof that the simplest, most humble-looking ingredients list can totally blow your mind. Whereas the Nonna Sauce on page 109 involves low-and-slow simmering over many hours, this recipe makes the most of fresh, in-season cherry tomatoes and takes only a couple of minutes to cook. Come July and August, when orange Sungold tomatoes are at their peak, I cook this pasta on repeat. Sungolds are just incredible when cooked gently. The soft bursts of sweet, garlicky nectar with a chunk of salt is god level.

This recipe is inspired by Chef Emilio Haynie, a real Buffalo bad boy. He taught me a very helpful trick for when it's not peak tomato season: Use half fresh tomatoes and half high-quality jarred tomatoes. I love La Catedral de Navarra brand. They are from Spain and have such beautiful sweetness and acidity. If you can find jarred yellow cherry tomatoes, pair them with fresh yellow cherry tomatoes. Another tip is to add a pat of butter if your tomatoes are not the greatest. This will temper the high acid on the unripe tomato and get you back into that cream-dream wheelhouse.

¾ pound dried spaghetti

3 tablespoons extra-virgin olive oil, plus more for drizzling

6 garlic cloves, thinly sliced

3½ cups baby Sungolds or other cherry tomatoes; half left whole, half sliced in half

1½ teaspoons kosher salt

Fresh basil leaves for topping

Freshly grated Parmigiano-Reggiano for topping

Flaky sea salt (such as Maldon)

1 Bring a large pot of salted water to a boil. Add the pasta and cook al dente according to the package directions.

2 While the pasta is cooking, in a large saucepan over medium heat, warm the 3 tablespoons olive oil. Add the garlic and sauté just until fragrant, about 45 seconds. Add all the cherry tomatoes and turn the heat to medium-high. Cook just until the tomatoes soften and most of them start to burst, 3 to 5 minutes. Turn the heat to low and season with the kosher salt.

3 Once the pasta is al dente, using tongs, transfer it directly into the saucepan and toss to coat, adding a ladleful of pasta water as needed to loosen the sauce and coat the pasta. Continue cooking over low heat until the tomatoes retain their shape but make a silky sauce that coats the threads of the pasta.

4 Transfer the pasta to individual serving bowls and top with fresh basil, Parm, sea salt, and a drizzle of olive oil. Serve immediately.

CHEF EMILIO

GARGANELLI
WITH RAGÙ

MAKES 4 TO 6 SERVINGS

½ cup diced pancetta

1 tablespoon extra-virgin olive oil

1 medium yellow onion, diced

2 large carrots, cut into ¼-inch dice

3 celery stalks, cut into ¼-inch dice

6 garlic cloves, minced

2½ tablespoons double-concentrated tomato paste

2 anchovy fillets

1 pound ground pork

½ pound ground beef (20% lean)

½ tablespoon freshly ground fennel seeds

½ tablespoon kosher salt

1 teaspoon freshly ground black pepper

¾ teaspoon red pepper flakes

1 cup dry white wine

3 cups chicken stock

½ cup milk

1½ pounds Fresh Egg Pasta (page 103) shaped into garganelli (see page 106), or 1 pound dried

1½ cups loosely packed finely grated Parmigiano-Reggiano, plus more for serving

2 tablespoons unsalted butter

continued

MAMA MIA, ME LIKEY RAGOOOOOUSHA!

These are the words that I scream through my house when I take my first bite of this dish. It's profound.

When we were in Modena, we had the opportunity for some deep Bologna hangouts, since the city was an easy 30 minutes away by train. Every night after shooting, we'd pop over to check out a different restaurant, and at almost every place we went, we'd order ragù Bolognese, the regional specialty. Soon I realized that every restaurant had their own different version—and every place would tell us that *theirs* was the true, authentic version. And every version was amazing!

That's what gave me the confidence to get a little experimental in developing my own Bolognese-style ragù. I've made the traditional version, which has ground veal in it and involves slow simmering for 4 or 5 hours. Don't get me wrong, it's amazing. But here, I skip the veal and cut the cooking time in half, closer to 2 hours. At that stage, the veg still has a bit of life to it, a bit more pop and snap. Don't sub bacon instead of pancetta. Two different worlds. Trust.

Don't be afraid to freeze a batch of this ragoush. It's the best quick meal. Reheat with a li'l butter and pasta water in the pan, and BOOM, it's better than the first time. If you don't feel up to making the garganelli from scratch, you can sub store-bought pasta (dried or fresh)—tagliatelle is a good choice.

1 Set a Dutch oven or a large, heavy-bottomed saucepan over medium-low heat. Add the pancetta and cook until crispy and the fat has mostly rendered out, about 7 minutes. Using a slotted spoon, transfer the pancetta to a plate and set aside. Add the olive oil to the pancetta fat and turn the heat to medium.

2 Add the onion, carrots, celery—this trifecta is called *soffritto* in Italian—and garlic to the pan. Cook, stirring occasionally, until the vegetables have softened, about 30 minutes. Push the mixture to one side of the pan. In the bare space, add the tomato paste and anchovy fillets and cook, stirring them, until the tomato paste is brick-red and very fragrant and the anchovies have dissolved, 1 minute. Now stir everything together.

3 Add the pork, beef, and reserved pancetta to the pan. Season with the ground fennel, salt, pepper, and red pepper flakes and stir to incorporate. Cook until the meat is brown and integrated, about 15 minutes. Use a wooden spoon to stir occasionally and break up the chunks of meat.

4 Turn the heat to medium-high and add the wine. Cook until the alcohol has evaporated and the pan is almost dry, about 5 minutes. Turn the heat to medium-low and add the chicken stock. Simmer for 1 hour, stirring occasionally. Mother the sauce, making sure that nothing sticks and burns on the bottom of the pot.

5 Turn the heat to low, add the milk, and let this ragù simmer for 20 minutes, stirring occasionally.

6 Meanwhile, bring a large pot of salted water to a boil. Add the pasta and cook al dente.

7 Stir 1 cup of the Parm and the butter into the ragù. (Note: If you want to save some ragù for later—either in the fridge or freezer—set it aside now, before you add the pasta.)

8 When the pasta is ready, drain and add it to the ragù, adding ½ cup of the pasta water if needed to loosen the sauce. Turn the heat to medium and cook, stirring, until the sauce is glossy and coats the pasta well. Taste and adjust the seasoning, adding the remaining ½ cup Parm, if needed. Transfer to individual bowls and top with a bit more Parm before serving.

Chef Life

All this pasta talk reminds me of a trip I took with John C. Reilly through Sicily. He was shooting a film over there and, between shoots, we'd travel up and down the coast searching for those real-deal premium bites. We were blown away by the distinct regional flavors of that beautiful island—the sweet Sicilian oranges, the special kind of basil they grow in Noto, the perfect raw red shrimp from Marzamemi, and the intense caperberries from Pantelleria. At restaurants, after one or two or three bottles of Etna wines, we'd always ask to see the chef to sing our praises of the meal. We'd bro out for a bit and then ask for a dining recommendation for the next town that we were scheduled to visit. Those tips were gold. Wherever chefs eat is usually where you can find the real shit.

Sicily is where John and I started calling each other "Chef," a tradition we hold to this day. It's our way of showing how much we honor and respect the craft of cooking. Our greeting to each other has actually transformed from "Hey Chef" to "Hey Ma Cheeeefer," but that's beside the point.

On one particularly wine-fueled evening at a fancy-pants spot in Taormina, we asked to see the chef after our beautiful meal. The restaurant proceeded to bring out not only the executive chef but also his sous chef, all the cooks, the pastry chef, AND the manager. In our broken Italian we tried to translate our joy with this experience. They nodded politely and probably thought, "Ugh, these annoying Americans. We have work to do!"

In the middle of John's gush fest about the pasta, a HUGE bug landed in his hair. I'm talking a bird-size, flying black thing. He stood up, screamed, and started to whip his hair back and forth to release the bug. It landed on the ground and skittered away. The restaurant team was in shock. Never had they seen a man yell so loudly and dance around in such horror in their five-star establishment. John tried to explain, "I received a bug in my hair." He acted out the flight path of the bug to help them understand, and at that moment I burst out in tears. Full cry-laughing. The kind of laughing where you are almost gagging to breathe. John burst into the same laughing fit. The kind that you know you will not recover from because it's all too ridiculous. We could not stop. The entire restaurant was staring. Then, one by one, the chefs and staff, confused by what they were seeing, walked away back to the kitchen. It was a glorious moment.

SEXY SCRAPS PASTA

MAKES 4 SERVINGS

1 tablespoon extra-virgin olive oil, plus ¼ cup

¼ cup panko bread crumbs; or day-old bread, pulsed in a food processor into coarse crumbs

¾ pound spaghetti (or whatever pasta looks good to you)

6 garlic cloves, thinly sliced

½ teaspoon red pepper flakes

Spring Scraps

8 ounces asparagus, trimmed and cut into 2-inch pieces

2 tablespoons medium caperberries, left whole, or small capers, drained

6 anchovy fillets

Kosher salt

¼ cup chopped parsley

Zest of 1 lemon

Freshly grated Parmigiano-Reggiano for finishing

Summer Scraps

2 tablespoons minced shallot

8 ounces summer squash, sliced into ¼-inch half-moons, or cherry tomatoes, halved (or a combo of the two)

Kosher salt

¼ cup chopped fresh mint or basil

Freshly grated Parmigiano-Reggiano for finishing

Scraps pasta isn't really a recipe . . . it's a state of mind. The idea is that whenever you have scraps of leftover veg in your fridge—a handful of kale, some cherry tomatoes, cauliflower, whatever!—you turn them into a sexy scraps pasta. It will take you 9 minutes, or however long it takes to boil your pasta, and costs, like, five dollars. If you follow the Heimy doctrine, you will always have bread crumbs, garlic, red pepper flakes, and olive oil in your pantry—those are the base ingredients, inspired by the simple and classic dish known as spaghetti aglio e olio (Italian for "garlic and oil"). From there, you can add whatever seasonal vegetables and complementary herbs you have on hand. You can really use whatever pasta you feel like here . . . I call for spaghetti, but I love linguine, tagliatelle, or even a wilder pasta shape, like sagna riccia. Scrap life is all about getting creative with what you've got.

1 In a small saucepan over medium-low, warm the 1 tablespoon olive oil. Add the bread crumbs and toast until evenly browned, about 1 minute. Transfer to a bowl and set aside.

2 Bring a large pot of salted water to a boil. Add the pasta and cook al dente, according to the package instructions.

3 Meanwhile, set a large saucepan over medium heat and warm the remaining ¼ cup olive oil. Add the garlic and red pepper flakes and sauté gently until the garlic begins to turn golden brown, 1 to 2 minutes. At this point, you have your base—now it's time to choose your scraps adventure.

4 *For Spring Scraps:* Add the asparagus, caperberries, anchovies, and a pinch of salt to the base and sauté until the asparagus turns bright green and is tender but still has plenty of snap, 3 to 5 minutes. Once the pasta is al dente, using tongs, transfer it directly into the saucepan and toss to coat, adding a bit of pasta water as needed to loosen the sauce and coat the pasta. Stir in the parsley, lemon zest, and plenty of Parm, then transfer to individual bowls. Serve immediately.

For Summer Scraps: Add the shallot to the base when you add the garlic. When golden, add the squash and/or tomatoes and a pinch of salt and sauté until softened and lightly browned, about 5 minutes. Once the pasta is al dente, using tongs, transfer it directly into the saucepan and toss to coat, adding a bit of pasta water as needed to loosen the sauce and coat the pasta. Stir in the mint and plenty of Parm, then transfer to individual bowls. Serve immediately.

For Autumn Scraps: Add the Broccolini and a pinch of salt to the base and stir to coat the veg in oil. Add a ladleful of pasta water to the pan, cover, and sauté-steam until the veg are bright green and tender but with a bit of bite, about 5 minutes. Once the pasta is al dente, using tongs, transfer it directly into the saucepan and toss to coat, adding a bit more pasta water as needed to loosen the sauce and coat the pasta. Stir in the parsley, lemon juice, and plenty of Pecorino, then transfer to individual bowls. Serve immediately.

Autumn Scraps

8 ounces Broccolini, cut into 3-inch pieces, or other cruciferous vegetable (quartered brussels sprouts, cauliflower cut into florets, etc.)

Kosher salt

¼ cup chopped parsley

Juice of ½ lemon, or to taste

Freshly grated Pecorino Romano for finishing

SEXY SCRAPS

TAGLIATELLE
WITH CHANTERELLES, CHILE, AND MINT

MAKES 4 SERVINGS

Mushrooms are so darn meaty and savory, and when you pair them with the contrasting zip of mint, chile, and lemon, you got yourself something very special. Chanterelles are like the champagne of mushrooms—an exquisite treat. If you can't find chanterelles, use another beautiful wild mushroom instead. Chanterelles have gills that get dirt stuck in them, so you may want to use a damp paper towel to clean them. Don't soak them in water because you want them dry for frying.

1 Tear any large mushrooms into bite-size pieces but leave a few smaller ones whole. They will shrink while cooking.

2 Bring a large pot of salted water to a boil. Add the pasta and cook al dente.

3 In a medium saucepan over high heat, warm the olive oil—you want to cook the mushrooms quickly and in a hot pan so they don't get mushy. Add the mushrooms, toss once or twice to get them coated in the frying fat, and cook until they are nicely browned and start to unstick from the pan, 4 to 5 minutes. Turn the heat to medium-low; add the butter, chile, garlic, red pepper flakes, a pinch of salt, and a few cranks of black pepper; and cook, stirring, until the ingredients are well integrated and the chile has softened, about 2 minutes.

4 Using tongs, transfer the pasta directly into the saucepan with the mushrooms. Toss to integrate the pasta and mushrooms, adding a bit of pasta water to loosen the sauce as needed. Stir in the mint and 1 cup Parm, turn the heat to low, and continue to cook until the sauce is glossy and the pasta is well coated, adding more pasta water if needed.

5 Remove the pasta from the heat, stir in the lemon juice (start with half and then add more to taste), and garnish with additional Parm and a few torn leaves of mint. Serve immediately.

10 ounces chanterelles or other wild mushrooms, cleaned

¾ pound Fresh Egg Pasta (page 103) shaped into tagliatelle (see page 106), or dried

¼ cup extra-virgin olive oil

¼ cup unsalted butter

1 Fresno or red jalapeño chile, stemmed, seeded (if desired), and thinly sliced

2 garlic cloves, thinly sliced

¼ teaspoon red pepper flakes

Kosher salt

Freshly ground black pepper

½ cup chopped mint, plus torn leaves for garnish

1 cup freshly grated Parmigiano-Reggiano, plus more for garnish

Juice of 1 lemon

AMALFI SUNSET PASTA

MAKES 4 SERVINGS

8 extra-large or jumbo
head-on, shell-on shrimp
or prawns

2 tablespoons unsalted butter

½ white onion, diced

3 garlic cloves, thinly sliced

1½ cups dry white wine

1½ cups whole canned
tomatoes, crushed by hand
or in a food mill

½ teaspoon red pepper flakes

Kosher salt

½ teaspoon freshly ground
black pepper

¾ pound dried linguine

1 teaspoon lemon juice

4 small basil leaves

Extra-virgin olive oil
for finishing

In Amalfi, you spend your days swimming under the hot Italian sun. After a short siesta, it's Sunset Spritz time, when you hop into a water taxi and find a cute cliffside restaurant where you can slurp seafood pasta seasoned with insane Amalfi lemons. Repeat this daily—until you max out your credit card and have to return to real life.

This recipe is my take on that classic Amalfi seafood pasta, but with a reduced seafood sauce that gives it a slight French vibe. It's essential to buy head-on, shell-on shrimp for this recipe—you're going to turn the heads and shells into a rich, briny stock that seasons the whole dish.

1 Twist the heads off the shrimp and peel off the shells, but don't toss away; you'll be using them soon to make a delicious sauce. Cut a small incision along the top edge of the shrimp, which should reveal a dark vein (unless the shrimp has already been purged). Using the tip of a paring knife, scrape away and discard the vein. (As an optional step, skewer each shrimp lengthwise on a toothpick so it doesn't curl too much during cooking.) Transfer the cleaned shrimp and the bowl with the heads and shells to the refrigerator.

2 Bring a large pot of salted water to a boil.

3 In a deep saucepan over medium heat, melt the butter. Add the onion and sauté until it is fragrant and lightly browned, 3 to 4 minutes. Add the garlic, shrimp heads and shells, wine, tomatoes, red pepper flakes, and 1 teaspoon salt and bring to a simmer. Partially cover the pan, turn the heat to medium-low, and continue to cook at a gentle simmer, stirring occasionally, until the tomatoes melt and the sauce is well integrated, about 20 minutes.

4 Remove the sauce from the heat and, using a fine-mesh sieve, strain out the solids, pressing the shells with a spoon to extract all the precious liquid. Return the sauce to the saucepan and season with salt and the black pepper—every shrimp is different, so it may be salty enough already! Keep the sauce warm over low heat.

5 Meanwhile, add the pasta to the boiling water and cook al dente according to the package directions.

6 Once the pasta is cooked, add the shrimp to the sauce and gently poach over low heat until they are pink and opaque—this should take about 1 minute. Remove the shrimp from the sauce so they don't overcook, then, using tongs, transfer the pasta into the saucepan. Add 2 tablespoons of the pasta water, or as much as needed to get the sauce to coat the pasta, and cook, stirring and tossing so that the pasta starts to absorb the sauce. Stir in the lemon juice.

7 Remove the pasta from the heat and divide evenly among four bowls. Place two shrimp and a basil leaf atop each bowl of pasta, then finish with a swirl of olive oil. Serve immediately.

7 In a large sauté pan over medium-high heat, warm the 3 tablespoons oil. Working in batches so as not to crowd the pan (if you jam them in too tightly, they'll steam rather than brown), deeply brown the rouladen on all sides. Transfer the browned rouladen to a plate and set aside.

8 To make the sauce: Add a splash more oil to the sauté pan if needed, then add the carrots, celeriac, leek, and onion and sauté over medium-high heat until they've browned, about 10 minutes. Season with salt, then add the tomato paste and cook for 2 minutes. Add a glug of the wine and deglaze the pan, making sure to scrape up all the delicious browned bits stuck to the bottom. Add the remaining wine and the beef broth and bring to a simmer, then cook until the vegetables are tender and the liquid has reduced, about 10 minutes.

9 Transfer the rouladen to a Dutch oven or a 9 by 13-inch roasting pan, then pour the sauce and vegetables over the top. (If needed, add up to 1 cup water so that the liquid comes halfway up the rouladen.) Cover the pan with a lid or aluminum foil and transfer to the oven.

10 Bake the rouladen for about 2 hours, checking every 30 minutes or so and spooning more sauce over the top. Flip the rouladen halfway through baking. (If the sauce is reducing too fast, lower the heat a touch and add more beef broth and water.)

11 Transfer the rouladen to a serving plate, then strain the vegetables out of the sauce by pouring it through a sieve into a bowl, pressing to extract all the delicious juices from the veg. Stir in the sour cream and season with salt and pepper.

12 Pour the sauce over the rouladen and serve immediately.

Note: If you're using flank steak, you'll need to ask your butcher to butterfly it lengthwise into two thin, flat pieces. Then you can cut those pieces into three even rectangles to yield six pieces.

DANKE, MUTTI!

BEEF BOURG
WITH PUREED POTATOES

MAKES 4 SERVINGS

This is one of my all-time fave wine meals. I usually get zero sleep the night before a Bourg—I'm too excited thinking about which wine I'm gonna pop that evening to pair with the succulent meat experience. Get a few bottles and a few friends and let the Bourg do the rest.

Make sure you have something decent to cook with too. You're going to use 2 cups of wine in the recipe, so pick out something that tastes nice—it doesn't have to be expensive. I like using a mineral-driven red for cooking. Nothing too jammy. I love Thierry Richoux's wines a lot. Grab 'em from The Source Imports.

Keep it ALL French ALL night. While I'm cooking, I put on some Serge Gainsbourg or Mr. Oizo (two French classics) and sip some crispy Chablis from Alice and Olivier de Moor or a refreshing Aligoté from Sylvain Pataille. Both wines are gorgeous and energizing. Set out a chunk of aged Comté for snick-snacks as well.

But when it comes to the main event, it's imperative to drink a beautiful red Burgundy. On my last Bourg night, we popped a bottle of 2016 "Les Damodes" from producer Chanterêves. Magnifique! Then a touch of Calvados at the end to settle everything up.

I recommend using a food mill for the potatoes. Once you puree potatoes with a food mill, you'll never go back to the masher technique. It's that ultra-soft, creamy sensation that gets me very excited and reminds me of the first bite I had of Joël Robuchon's famous potatoes in Paris.

Now, let's BOURG.

1 Preheat your oven to 325°F. Line a paper plate with a double layer of paper towels.

2 In a Dutch oven or a large, ovenproof, heavy-bottomed saucepan over medium-low heat, warm the 1 teaspoon oil. Add the bacon and cook until crispy, 10 to 12 minutes. Using a slotted spoon, transfer to the prepared plate to drain.

3 Pat the beef dry with paper towels (this is important—wet beef won't brown properly) and season with salt and pepper. Add the beef to the pot with the bacon drippings, turn the heat to medium, and, working in batches as necessary (you don't want to crowd the pan—each beef piece should get a bit of room), cook until the meat is browned on all sides, 10 to 12 minutes. Transfer the beef to a plate and set aside.

4 Add the onion, carrots, and garlic to the pan and cook, stirring and occasionally scraping the bottom of the pan, until the onion has softened, about 7 minutes. Add the beef and its drippings back to the pan.

1 teaspoon neutral oil

4 slices bacon, cut into 1-inch pieces

2 pounds beef stew meat (see Note), cut into 2-inch cubes

Kosher salt and freshly ground black pepper

1 yellow onion, quartered and thinly sliced

5 small or 2 large carrots, peeled and cut into 1-inch chunks

2 garlic cloves, minced

2 tablespoons all-purpose flour

2 cups red wine (preferably Burgundy)

2 to 3 cups beef stock

1 tablespoon tomato paste

2 sprigs thyme

2 bay leaves

Pureed Potatoes

2½ pounds large potatoes (such as Yukon gold), peeled and quartered

Kosher salt

6 tablespoons unsalted butter

¾ cup heavy cream, or as needed

Freshly ground white pepper

½ cup fresh or frozen pearl onions

1 tablespoon salted butter

1 tablespoon neutral oil, plus 1 teaspoon

2 cups quartered cremini mushrooms

¼ cup chopped fresh parsley

continued

5 Sprinkle the flour over the beef and stir to coat and cook the flour slightly, 1 to 2 minutes. Add the wine and enough of the beef stock to barely cover the meat. (If you're using fancy short rib rather than a cheaper stew meat, add a bit less stock, as your cook time will be shorter.) Add half of the reserved bacon, the tomato paste, thyme, and bay leaves. Crumble the remaining bacon and save it for garnish.

6 Cover the pan and transfer to the oven. Cook for 2 to 3 hours, stirring gently every 30 minutes or so, until the beef is extremely tender and easily pierced with a fork. After the liquid has started to reduce, at around the 1-hour mark, check for seasoning and adjust with salt and pepper as needed.

7 To make the potatoes: While the beef is cooking, place the potatoes in a medium pot, cover with water, and season with plenty of salt. Bring to a boil and cook until the potatoes are tender and very easily pierced with a knife, 15 to 20 minutes. Drain the potatoes.

8 If you have a food mill, mill the potatoes and transfer them back into the warm pot. Alternatively, transfer the potatoes back to the warm pot and mash with a potato masher or fork. Stir in the butter and cream, adding more as needed to get a nice, smooth consistency. Season with salt and white pepper. Keep warm.

9 Meanwhile, set a sauté pan over medium-low heat; add the pearl onions, butter, and 1 tablespoon oil; and cook until browned, about 10 minutes. Transfer the onions to a plate and set aside. Reserve the cooking fat in the pan.

10 In the same pan, combine the mushrooms, remaining 1 teaspoon oil, and 1 tablespoon water. Cook, stirring, until the mushrooms have softened and browned, about 5 minutes. Transfer the mushrooms to the plate with the onions.

11 Once the beef is super-tender and the sauce has reduced by about a third—it should have the consistency of a nice gravy—remove it from the oven and gently stir in the pearl onions and mushrooms. Serve over the potatoes and sprinkle with the parsley and the remainder of the bacon crumbles as garnish.

Note: For the beef, you can use chuck or any stew meat—it's supposed to be a rustic dish. But if you are feeling fancy, use bottom round or even short rib for an elevated experience. Nicer cuts don't need to cook as long to reach tenderness, so plan to shorten the total cook time by about 30 minutes.

nice

NAUGHTY 'N' NICE MEATBALLS
(CREAM BALLS AND POLPETTE)

MAKES ABOUT 20 MEATBALLS (4 SERVINGS)

Meatballs

2 tablespoons extra-virgin olive oil

½ yellow onion, finely diced

½ pound ground beef

½ pound ground pork

1 egg

¼ cup milk

½ cup bread crumbs

2 tablespoons chopped flat-leaf parsley

2 garlic cloves, grated

1½ teaspoons freshly ground fennel seeds

1½ teaspoons kosher salt

1 teaspoon freshly ground black pepper

"Nice" Version

½ cup extra-virgin olive oil

Chopped fresh parsley for garnish

"Naughty" Version

¼ cup unsalted butter

¼ cup all-purpose flour

2 cups beef broth

½ cup white wine

1 egg yolk

¼ cup sour cream

¼ cup capers, drained

Juice of ½ lemon

1 teaspoon kosher salt

Freshly ground black pepper

When Circle Foods and Grandma Foods intersect, deliciousness happens. That's why meatballs are so spectacular. And why I decided to offer *two* versions.

The "nice" version is pan-fried in a bit of olive oil. In Italy, they call these "polpette" and serve them straight up, no sauce, at room temp as an appetizer. (When I'm feeling a li'l *Goodfellas*, I go the Italian American route and let my meatballs take a dip in tomato-y Nonna Sauce [page 109]. Serve this with some garlic bread on the side—marone!)

When I'm feeling frisky, that's when the craving for richer, German-inspired cream balls hits. These aren't pan-fried at all; they cook straight in the sauce, resulting in a fluffier meatball experience. Serve with some boiled potatoes on the side for a cream-dream circle experience.

1 To make the meatballs: In a medium skillet over medium heat, warm the olive oil, then add the onion and sauté until it is translucent, about 5 minutes. Set aside to cool slightly.

2 In a large bowl, combine the cooled onion with the beef, pork, egg, milk, bread crumbs, parsley, garlic, fennel seeds, salt, and pepper and mix by hand until well incorporated. Form the mixture into 1½-inch balls and set aside on plates or a baking sheet.

3 *For the "nice" version:* In a large cast-iron skillet over medium-low heat, warm the olive oil. Test for seasoning by tearing off and frying a small piece from one of the meatballs. Eat your tester and adjust the seasoning as needed.

Working in batches so as not to crowd the pan, fry the meatballs, rotating every minute or so to brown all sides (lean the balls on each other to get the right angles), about 8 minutes. The meatballs should be crisp on the outside and juicy on the inside (cut one in half to test). Garnish with parsley before serving.

For the "naughty" version: In a Dutch oven or a large, heavy-bottomed saucepan over medium heat, melt the butter. Add the flour and immediately start whisking vigorously. Cook, whisking continuously, until the mixture is a light golden color, 2 to 3 minutes.

Slowly pour the beef broth into the flour mixture, while whisking, until the sauce is well integrated, then stir in the wine. Bring to a low simmer and cook until the sauce has thickened slightly, stirring occasionally and making sure to scrape the bottom, about 10 minutes.

Add the meatballs to the sauce and return to a low simmer. Cover the pan, turn the heat to low, and cook until the meatballs are cooked through (cut one in half to test), 15 to 20 minutes.

Using a slotted spoon, transfer the meatballs to a serving bowl, then remove the sauce from the heat. In a small bowl, whisk together the egg yolk, sour cream, and capers. Add to the sauce and stir to combine.

Season the sauce with the lemon juice, salt, and a sprinkling of pepper, then pour over the meatballs and serve. No garnish here—EMBRACE THE BEIGE!

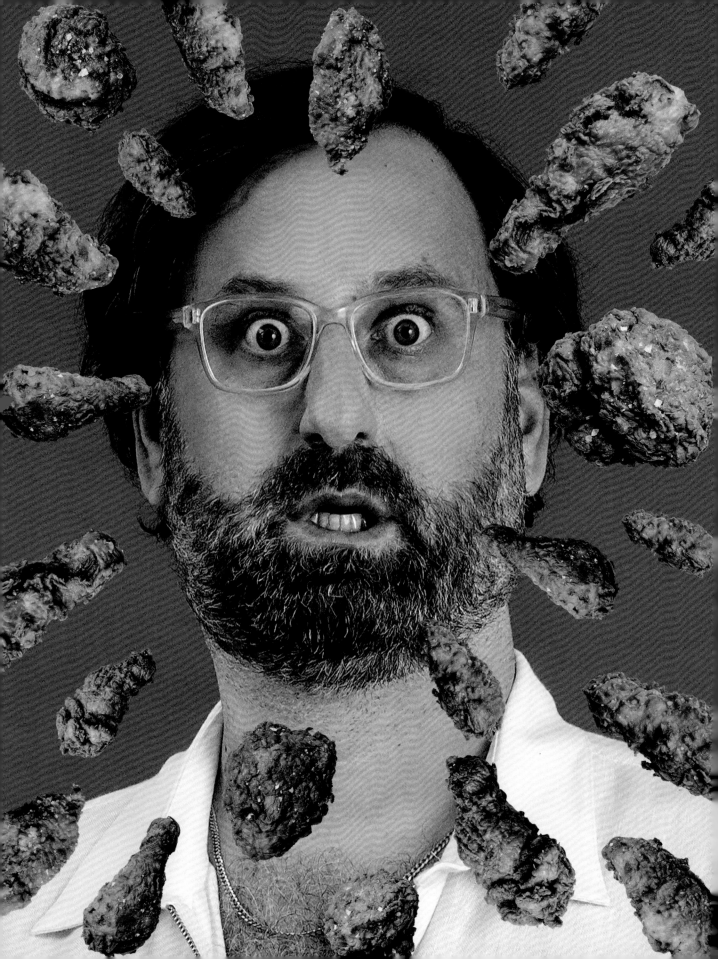

I love a dang bird. But unlike your average American tot, I didn't grow up with nuggets and tenderinis—my chicken conversion came later in life. My mom didn't really cook tons of chicken at home, apart from the occasional chicken paprikash. It was only when I started touring the country that I had truly transcendent chicken experiences. And more often than not, that chicken was fried. Hot chicken in Nashville. Chicken wings at T-Pain's strip club in Atlanta. Classic Southern fried chicken at Babes outside of Dallas, and Willie Mae's in New Orleans. The list goes on and on and on.

There's a roast chicken in this chapter, which is bronzed and beautiful and I definitely want you to try it. But other than that, you're in Fry Town, baby. My devotion to crisp extends to many foods, but especially to chicken. There's some kind of magical alchemy that happens when yummy chickers hit that hot oil.

In this chapter and throughout the book, I ask you to do a fair amount of frying. Why? Because frying makes all food taste magical. If you've never fried at home, here are a few tips to get it right.

- Fry in good-quality neutral oil with a high smoke point. I really like peanut oil, which is traditional in the South, but canola and grapeseed oil are good too.

- Be careful with hot oil. In my early fry life, I splashed oil all over the place and burned the heck out of my hand. Use a deep pot with tall sides to catch splatter, and never fill it more than a third of the way with oil. Make sure anything that touches hot oil (pot, spoon, thermometer) is totally dry. Water will make the oil spit like the dickens.

- Set up a sheet pan with a wire rack on top of it to place just-fried food.

- Always season with salt the minute your food comes out of the hot oil.

- Once the cooking oil has cooled completely, you can use a strainer and funnel to carefully pour it back into its container and reuse it later.

- When your oil is ready to be tossed, make sure it's completely cool, then dump it into a plastic garbage bag, tie it up securely, and toss in the trash.

naughty

NAUGHTY 'N' NICE FRIED CHICKEN

MAKES 4 TO 6 SERVINGS

Buttermilk Brine

3½ cups buttermilk

¾ cup hot sauce
(preferably Crystal brand)

6 garlic cloves, minced

6 tablespoons
cayenne pepper

¼ cup kosher salt

2 tablespoons black pepper

1½ tablespoons garlic powder

1 tablespoon smoked paprika

One 5-pound whole chicken,
butchered (see Note)

Coating

4 cups all-purpose flour

1½ tablespoons kosher salt

2 cups buttermilk

¾ cup hot sauce
(preferably Crystal brand)

Peanut oil or other neutral oil
for frying

Kosher salt

1 lemon, cut into wedges,
for serving "nice" style

Naughty Sauce (recipe
follows) for serving
"naughty" style

Atlanta taught me a lot about fried chicken. I used to visit all the time since the Adult Swim network is located there. Mike Lazzo, Adult Swim's head honcho, would always host biz lunches at real-deal barbecue joints or chicken shacks—such a far cry from my annoying meetings in Los Angeles, surrounded by suits and plastic-surgery freaks. But Atlanta has so much heart and soul. The first time a local called me "Hunny Bun," I almost passed out from the warm, happy feeling that tingled through my body.

On my most recent visit to Atlanta, some friends and I decided to do three fried chickens in a row—a fried-chicken trifecta. (Of course, we came packing ice-cold dry Riesling and Chablis.) We started at the Colonnade, an old-school restaurant that's been open since 1927; then we went to Revival, a legit newer spot run by legend Kevin Gillespie; and we ended at a strip club called Magic City. Each spot was bonk and had its own unique fried-chicken preparation, but I think Magic City's was the best. Or maybe it's a tie with T-Pain's wings at Onyx. My next book should be *Strip Club Wangs: The Complete Guidebook*.

All of this chicken beauty inspired me to create my Naughty 'n' Nice Fried Chicken, which is really two recipes in one. The "nice" version is served very simply, with lemon wedges on the side—a nod to Japanese-style karaage that I loved so much in Tokyo. The "naughty version" is kind of a mash-up of Atlanta chicken and the hot chicken served at iconic Nashville restaurant Prince's. Mine is a bit different than the Nashville style, which, while delicious, is crazy spicy and (at least for me) a bit painful to eat. In Atlanta, they often serve fried chicken with honey and hot sauce on the side, so I decided to combine that into a sweet 'n' spicy drizzle.

For both preparations, you'll have this really flavorful meat due to the spicy brine. If you have a cleaver and decent knife skills, you can butcher the chicken yourself—or just ask the person behind the meat counter to cut the whole bird into pieces for you.

1 To make the brine: In a bowl large enough to hold all the chicken pieces, combine the buttermilk, hot sauce, garlic, cayenne, salt, black pepper, garlic powder, and paprika and stir to incorporate.

2 Submerge the chicken pieces in the brine, cover the bowl with plastic wrap, and let marinate in the refrigerator for at least 6 hours or up to 24 hours.

3 To prepare the coating: In a large bowl, whisk together the flour and salt. In a separate bowl, stir together the buttermilk and hot sauce.

4 Set a rack on top of a baking sheet.

5 Working with one piece at a time, remove the chicken from the brine and let any excess drip off. Dip the piece of chicken in the flour mixture to coat, making sure to get flour in every nook and cranny, and shake off the excess. Dip into the buttermilk mixture, allowing any excess to drip off. Return the piece to the flour mixture and again make sure every bit of the surface of the chicken is coated in flour. Transfer to the prepared rack.

6 Once all of the chicken is coated, fill a large Dutch oven with enough peanut oil to fully submerge the chicken pieces and heat to 335°F. Set another rack over a baking sheet to hold your cooked chicken.

7 Working in batches so as not to overcrowd the Dutch oven, fry the chicken until the coating is a deep golden brown and the internal temperature is 160°F, 6 to 8 minutes for smaller pieces, like the drumettes and legs, and 8 to 10 minutes for larger pieces. (Keep an eye on the color of the fry—that is your best doneness cue.) Make sure to wait a bit in between batches to let the frying oil come back up to temperature; if your oil temperature is too low, the chicken will take longer to fry and be greasy. As each piece finishes frying, transfer it to the prepared rack to drain and then season with salt. (Reserve ¾ cup of the frying oil if making Naughty Sauce.) Once all the chicken is fried, arrange it on a serving platter.

8 If you're feeling nice, simply scatter the lemon wedges around the chicken and squeeze some lemon juice on each piece before eating. If you're feeling naughty, drizzle the Naughty Sauce all over the chicken and be prepared for some sweet 'n' spicy bites!

Note: Ask your butcher to cut the chicken into eight pieces (wings, breasts, thighs, and drumsticks), then ask them to cut each breast into three bone-in pieces (or, if your bird is smaller than 5 pounds, cut them into two pieces), and each thigh into two bone-in pieces (or, if your bird is smaller than 5 pounds, leave them whole). Finally, ask them to separate the drumettes from the wing tips and flats (you can discard the wing tips and flats, or save them for stock).

In a medium bowl, whisk together the honey, cayenne, chipotle powder, and paprika. Pour in ½ cup of the reserved frying oil, then whisk to combine. Add more oil as needed to achieve your desired runny consistency. Serve immediately.

NAUGHTY SAUCE

MAKES ABOUT 1 CUP

½ cup honey

1 tablespoon cayenne pepper

1 tablespoon chipotle powder

1 tablespoon smoked paprika

¾ cup reserved frying oil

MUTTI'S CHICKEN SCHNITZEL
WITH CAPER-LEMON BUTTER AND CHIVE POTATOES

MAKES 4 SERVINGS

Here's another classic from my childhood—crispy schnitz with pillow-soft taters. It's a simple schnitz base, but the caper-lemon butter elevates it in the best way. Remember my chicken mantra: Happy chickens, happy dish. Buy good, organic chicken breasts that are on the smaller side—no mutant, antibiotic-pumped birds, please. I take the extra step of cutting off the tender from the breast and frying that separately—save it for a tasty treat (see "Heimy's Hint," page 150).

Growing up, we used to eat this with rotkraut, a German red cabbage dish that is akin to sauerkraut but way less sour and intense. You can find jars of rotkraut at European specialty food stores.

Four 6-ounce boneless, skinless chicken breasts

Kosher salt and freshly ground black pepper

1 cup all-purpose flour

2 eggs

½ cup milk

3½ cups fine plain bread crumbs

2 pounds red creamer potatoes, halved or quartered

¼ cup chopped fresh chives

7 tablespoons unsalted butter

Neutral oil for frying

2 tablespoons capers, drained

Juice of 1 lemon, plus ½ lemon, cut into wedges

1 Bring a large pot of salted water to a boil, set two wire racks on top of two baking sheets, and preheat your oven to 200°F.

2 Place a layer of parchment paper or plastic wrap on your work surface, then place a chicken breast on top and cover the chicken with another layer of parchment or plastic. Using a kitchen mallet or a rolling pin, pound the chicken to ¼ inch thick. It should be super-thin, but if the flesh starts tearing, stop pounding—you've gone far enough. Repeat with the remaining chicken breasts. Season each chicken breast with salt and pepper.

3 Place the flour in a large bowl and stir in 3 teaspoons salt and 1 teaspoon pepper. Crack the eggs into another large bowl, add the milk, and beat lightly with a fork. Place half of the bread crumbs in a third large bowl (refreshing with additional bread crumbs as needed throughout the dredging process).

4 Working with one piece at a time, dip both sides of the chicken into the flour, making sure to get flour in every nook and cranny, then shake off any excess. Dip into the egg mixture, allowing any excess to drip off. Then dip into the bread crumbs, coating both sides and pressing to make sure the bread crumbs really coat the surface of the chicken. Transfer to the prepared rack.

5 Place the potatoes in the boiling water and cook until they are fork-tender, about 15 minutes. Drain, then while the potatoes are still warm, toss with the chives and 1 tablespoon of the butter and season liberally with salt and pepper. Keep warm.

6 Fill a Dutch oven or a large, heavy-bottomed saucepan with enough oil to come halfway up the sides of the chicken breasts and warm over medium-high heat. The target temperature is 335°F, drop a bit of bread crumbs into the pan to test whether the oil is hot enough (it should sizzle).

continued

7 Add one or two chicken breasts at a time, depending on the size of your pan, and making sure not to overcrowd the pan, and fry until deep golden brown, 6 to 8 minutes, flipping halfway. Transfer to the second prepared baking sheet, season with salt, and place in the oven to keep warm as you cook the remaining chicken breasts.

8 In a small, cold saucepan, combine 1 tablespoon butter and the capers. Set over medium-high heat and cook until the butter is melted and the capers are fragrant, about 1 minute. Add the lemon juice and turn the heat to a simmer. Cook until the sauce has reduced a bit, about 2 minutes. Turn off the heat and then immediately whisk in the remaining 5 tablespoons butter.

9 Place each chicken breast onto individual plates and spoon the caper-lemon butter over the tops. Spoon some potatoes onto each plate, adjust the seasoning with salt and pepper as needed, and garnish with a lemon wedge. Serve immediately.

Heimy's Hint

Cut a small, dinner roll–size King's Hawaiian roll in half, schmear both cut sides with mayonnaise (Japanese brand Kewpie is best), season with a bit of salt and fresh black pepper, then sandwich a chicken tender in the middle and douse with a healthy splash of Tabasco. There's a lot of fun in that bun!

CHICKEN PARM

MAKES 4 SERVINGS

This chicken Parm is the Italian American cousin of my German schnitzy. It takes me back to my college days in Philly, where so many of our fave restaurants were red-sauce joints. But once you try this recipe and taste the insane flavor of my sauce paired with that super-crispy primo chicken and molten mozz, I guarantee you'll start doing those red-sauce nights at your house instead. Pair this with high-altitude Nebbiolo from Carema. Producer Luigi Ferrando's wines are gorgeous.

Four 6-ounce boneless, skinless chicken breasts

Kosher salt and freshly ground black pepper

1 cup all-purpose flour

2 eggs

½ cup milk

3½ cups panko bread crumbs

Neutral oil for frying

2 cups Nonna Sauce (page 109), or as needed

1½ cups shredded low-moisture mozzarella

¼ cup freshly grated Parmigiano-Reggiano, plus more for finishing

Fresh basil leaves for finishing

1 Have ready two baking sheets; set a wire rack on top of one.

2 Place a layer of parchment paper or plastic wrap on your work surface, then place a chicken breast on top and cover the chicken with another layer of parchment or plastic. Using a kitchen mallet or a rolling pin, pound the chicken to just over ¼ inch. Repeat with the remaining chicken breasts. Season each chicken breast with salt and pepper.

3 Place the flour in a large bowl and stir in 3 teaspoons salt and 1 teaspoon pepper. Crack the eggs into another large bowl, add the milk, and beat lightly with a fork. Place half of the panko in a third large bowl (refreshing with additional panko as needed throughout the dredging process).

4 Working with one piece at a time, dip both sides of the chicken into the flour, making sure to get flour in every nook and cranny, then shake off any excess. Dip into the egg mixture, allowing any excess to drip off. Then dip into the panko, coating both sides and pressing to make sure the panko really coats the surface of the chicken. Transfer to the prepared rack.

5 Fill a Dutch oven or a large, heavy-bottomed saucepan with enough oil to come halfway up the sides of the chicken breasts and warm over medium-high heat. The target temperature is 335°F, drop a bit of panko into the pan to test whether the oil is hot enough (it should sizzle).

6 Add one or two chicken breasts at a time, depending on the size of your pan, and making sure not to overcrowd the pan, and fry until deep golden brown, 6 to 8 minutes, flipping halfway. Transfer to the second baking sheet and set aside as you cook the remaining chicken breasts.

7 Arrange a rack in the center of your oven and preheat the broiler.

8 Evenly spread about ⅓ cup of the sauce over the top of each chicken piece. Sprinkle one-fourth of the mozz over that and then sprinkle 1 tablespoon of the Parm over the mozz.

9 Place the chicken in the oven and broil for 3 to 5 minutes, keeping a very close eye on things—this can go from perfectly melted to burned in the blink of an eye. Remove when the cheese is bubbly and golden brown.

10 Using a spatula, carefully transfer each piece of chicken to individual plates. Finish with a little more Parm and a few leaves of basil. Serve with any remaining Nonna Sauce in a small bowl at the table, in case anyone needs extra.

ORANGE CHICKEN

MAKES 4 SERVINGS

2 eggs

1 cup cornstarch

½ cup all-purpose flour

Kosher salt and freshly
ground white pepper

2 pounds boneless, skinless
chicken thighs, cut into
bite-size pieces

Neutral oil for frying

Orange Sauce

1 tablespoon neutral oil

2 garlic cloves, minced

1-inch knob ginger, minced

½ teaspoon red pepper flakes

⅔ cup fresh orange juice,
plus more as needed

2 tablespoons fresh
lemon juice

2 tablespoons soy sauce,
plus more as needed

1 tablespoon unseasoned
rice vinegar

1 tablespoon Sriracha,
plus more as needed

1 tablespoon hoisin sauce

1 tablespoon packed dark
brown sugar, plus more
as needed

1 tablespoon cornstarch

2 tablespoons water

Cooked white rice for serving

2 green onions, thinly sliced

Sesame seeds for garnish

1 orange, cut into wedges

The orange chicken from Panda Express was one of my first food crushes. Cravings still hit, even today. . . . Usually it's late-night and I find myself Googling "panda express near me." But then I catch myself and realize I'm being a bad boy and I don't want a stomachache and I can make an amazing version at home, using happy chickens and tons of fresh ginger and fresh orange juice. These days I forgo the Mountain Dew and instead pair my orange chicken with a crisp Riesling. The long, salty finish of the wine with this deep, dank citrus sauce is what I live for.

1 Set two wire racks on top of two baking sheets.

2 In a large bowl, lightly beat the eggs with a fork. In a separate large bowl, combine the 1 cup cornstarch and the flour and season with a pinch each of salt and white pepper. Season the chicken with salt and white pepper, then coat the pieces in the egg, toss them in the cornstarch mixture, and shake to remove any excess. Transfer to a prepared rack and set aside.

3 In a Dutch oven or a large, heavy-bottomed saucepan over medium-high heat, warm 1 inch of oil to 350°F. Working in batches so as not to crowd the pan, add the chicken and fry until it is cooked through and crispy, 5 to 7 minutes. Transfer to the second rack to drain.

4 To make the sauce: In a medium saucepan over medium heat, warm the oil. Add the garlic, ginger, and red pepper flakes and sauté just until aromatic, 1 to 2 minutes. Add the ⅔ cup orange juice, the lemon juice, 2 tablespoons soy sauce, vinegar, 1 tablespoon Sriracha, hoisin, and 1 tablespoon brown sugar; stir to combine; and bring to a simmer. Taste and adjust the seasoning if needed. If you feel the sauce needs to be juicier, add a bit more orange juice; saltier, add a bit more soy sauce; spicier, add a bit more Sriracha; sweeter, add a bit more brown sugar.

5 In a small bowl, whisk together the 1 tablespoon cornstarch with the water. Slowly drizzle this into the sauce, whisking gently to combine, and continue to simmer until the sauce has thickened into a syrupy but still pourable glaze, about 3 minutes more.

6 In a mixing bowl, coat the fried chicken pieces with the sauce.

7 Divide the rice among four bowls, top with the chicken, and garnish with the green onions and sesame seeds. Serve with orange wedges on the side.

CHICKEN TOWER
WITH HERB OVERLOAD

MAKES 2 OR 3 SERVINGS

Poaching Liquid

6 cups water

Juice of ½ lemon

½ yellow onion, chopped

¾ cup chopped ginger

3 garlic cloves, smashed

1 teaspoon kosher salt

1 teaspoon freshly ground
black pepper

½ teaspoon red pepper flakes

2 boneless skinless chicken
breasts

Nước Chấm

½ cup water

¼ cup fish sauce, or to taste

¼ cup lime juice

2 tablespoons rice wine vinegar

1 tablespoon grated palm
sugar or granulated sugar

1 garlic clove, minced

½ bird's eye chile, minced

4 medium carrots, julienned
and cut into 2-inch-long pieces

½ head cabbage, cored and
shredded

½ red onion, thinly sliced

1 tablespoon chopped cilantro,

1 tablespoon chopped mint

1 tablespoon crushed peanuts

Crispy Garlic (recipe follows)

This is the most refreshing salad ever, with a bright dressing inspired by nước chấm, a classic Vietnamese dipping sauce. Vietnamese food is near and dear to Heimy's heart, and figuring out how to make this was a revelation. It's simple and gives you such good energy. When I'm shooting, this is the lunch that will give me pep in my step to finish up the funnies for the day. One of the most essential elements here is fish sauce. If you haven't cooked with it before, it's deliciously funky. It's also intense—and there is a fair amount of variation between brands—so add it gradually and keep tasting until you reach a level you like.

This recipe has you poach chicken breasts, but you can also use leftover chicken. Roasted or rotisserie, it's all good. Be careful when you're handling bird's eye chiles—these suckers are hot! Wash your hands really well after cutting them. Then wash them again. And wash a third time before you touch your intimate parts!

❶ To make the poaching liquid: In a Dutch oven or a deep pot, combine the water, lemon juice, yellow onion, ginger, garlic, salt, pepper, and red pepper flakes. Bring to a boil, then lower the heat and let simmer until the flavors have infused, about 15 minutes.

❷ Meanwhile, fill a large bowl with ice cubes and water to prepare an ice bath.

❸ Lower the heat again so the poaching liquid is just below a simmer. You want it as hot as it can get without bubbling. Add the chicken breasts and cook until the juices run clear and an instant-read thermometer registers 160°F, 15 to 17 minutes (more or less, depending on the thickness of the chicken), flipping the breasts halfway. Immediately transfer the chicken to the ice bath. Once cooled, use a fork to shred into bite-size pieces.

❹ To make the nước chấm: In a medium bowl, combine the water, fish sauce, lime juice, vinegar, sugar, garlic, and chile and stir to incorporate. Taste and adjust the seasoning as needed. It should balance funky, sweet, and sour.

❺ In a large bowl, combine the carrots, cabbage, and red onion and pour about half of the nước chấm over the top. Transfer to a large serving bowl or divide between individual plates and top each serving with the shredded chicken, cilantro, mint, peanuts, crispy garlic, and more nước chấm to taste. Serve immediately.

CRISPY GARLIC

MAKES 2 TABLESPOONS GARLIC
AND ¼ CUP GARLIC OIL

6 garlic cloves, thinly sliced

¼ cup neutral oil

In a small, cold saucepan, combine the garlic and oil. Set over medium heat and fry just until light golden, about 3 minutes—if you go too long, the garlic will become bitter. Once golden, strain the garlic and drain on paper towels. Store in the refrigerator for up to 1 week.

PARISIAN CHICKEN
WITH MUSHROOM SAUCE AND FRENCH FRIES

MAKES 4 SERVINGS

It's hard for me to think of a more perfect meal than the simple roast chicken with french fries I had at Le Repaire de Cartouche in Paris, a restaurant run by the legendary Rodolphe Paquin. Rodolphe has one of the coolest cellars in Paris, so his food is intentionally unfussy, to allow the wine to shine through. I'll never forget eating his chicken and dipping fries in this silky, umami-rich mushroom sauce while drinking a bottle of Philippe Jambon's La Grande Bruyère, a Chardonnay made from grapes grown in Mâcon.

A classic French thing to do (and something I highly recommend) is to spend Sunday with your friends drinking good wine and then eating a roast chicken with french fries for a late lunch. This is such a versatile dish to pair with wine, and it works with white wine and light reds. If you want to stay in France, try Chardonnay from Burgundy or Chenin Blanc from the Loire Valley for white wine, or Gamay from Beaujolais or Poulsard from the Jura for a lighter-weight red.

To get the timing right, so you have hot fries ready once you've carved the bird, I recommend heating the frying oil before the bird goes in the oven (this can take a while), then start the first fry as soon as you put the chicken in the oven. Let the fries hang out draining on paper towels while the chicken cooks, then get a buddy to do the second fry while you're making the mushroom sauce. It's a two-person job BUT it ensures you have hot fries when you're ready to eat!

One 3- to 4-pound whole chicken

Kosher salt

Extra-virgin olive oil for drizzling

1 handful mixed fresh herbs (thyme, rosemary, marjoram, or tarragon), tied together with butcher's twine

7 garlic cloves; 4 smashed, 3 thinly sliced

1 cup white wine

1 tablespoon unsalted butter

1 shallot, diced

8 cremini mushrooms, thinly sliced

Freshly ground black pepper

1 tablespoon all-purpose flour

½ cup heavy cream

1 batch French Fries (recipe follows)

1. Preheat your oven to 475°F.

2. Allow the chicken to come to room temperature before cooking. If the chicken comes packaged with giblets, discard the giblets (or freeze them for gravy). Forty-five minutes before you plan to roast the chicken, season it all over with salt—make sure to get inside the cavity too—to allow the salt time to draw out excess moisture from the skin. Place the chicken breast-side up on the rack of a roasting pan and wick away any excess moisture with paper towels.

3. Drizzle a bit of olive oil over the herbs and then place the herbs and smashed garlic in the cavity of the chicken. Truss the chicken by tying its legs together so they don't splay open. Keep it classy!

4. Place the chicken in the oven and roast for 25 minutes, rotating the bird once halfway through, then turn the oven temperature to 325°F. Continue cooking until the juices run clear when the chicken is pierced with a paring knife, another 20 to 30 minutes, depending on the size of your bird. (If the skin looks like it's starting to burn or if the breast is close to doneness

continued

before the thighs and legs are ready, cover the hot spots with aluminum foil to slow down cooking.) Remove from the oven when an instant-read thermometer inserted into the thickest part of the breast reads 150°F and the thigh reads 160°F. (This is lower than the USDA guidelines . . . but remember, the chicken will keep cooking once you take it out of the oven and may go up an additional 5° to 10°F.) Transfer to a cutting board, cover loosely with foil, and allow to rest for 15 minutes.

5 Place the roasting pan with the chicken drippings over medium heat. Add the wine and deglaze the pan, using a wooden spoon to scrape up any of the tasty, crusty bits stuck to the bottom. Once the brown bits have been loosened, about 1 minute, remove the pan from the heat and set aside.

6 In a separate sauté pan over medium-low heat, melt the butter. Add the shallot and sauté until translucent, about 2 minutes. Add the mushrooms and cook until they are browned and soft, about 5 minutes more. Add the sliced garlic, a pinch of salt, and a generous crank of black pepper and cook until fragrant, about 30 seconds. Add the reserved deglazing liquid, stir to combine, sprinkle the flour evenly over the mushrooms, and stir again to combine. Once the flour gains some color, add the cream and cook until incorporated, about 5 minutes. Season with salt and pepper as needed.

7 Carve the chicken and transfer to a serving plate. Transfer the sauce to a serving bowl to pass alongside the chicken and french fries. Start dippin' those fries!

FRENCH FRIES

MAKES 4 SERVINGS

2½ pounds russet potatoes, scrubbed clean but not peeled

Neutral oil for frying

Kosher salt

1 Cut the potatoes into ½-inch batons, about 3 inches long. As you cut them, transfer to a bowl of ice water to release some of the starch and keep them from oxidizing.

2 Fill a Dutch oven or a large, heavy-bottomed saucepan with 3 to 4 inches of oil and heat to 325°F. Set a wire rack on top of a baking sheet. Line a bowl with a clean, dry towel or paper towels.

3 Working in two or three batches, add the potatoes to the oil—make sure the potatoes can swim around comfortably and aren't clumping together—and cook until they just begin to brown, about 4 minutes. Using a spider skimmer or slotted spoon, transfer the fries to the prepared baking sheet to drain. (The potatoes can rest like this for about 30 minutes.)

4 When you're ready for the second fry, increase the temperature of the oil to 375°F. Again, working in two or three batches so as not to crowd the pot, re-fry the potatoes, this time until they're nicely browned and crispy, 3 to 4 minutes. Transfer to the prepared bowl, season liberally with salt, and toss to coat. Serve immediately.

"THE JOY OF JUICE"
A food poem by Eric Wareheim

When you're in Tuscany and grab the bone
from your bistecca alla fiorentina to gnaw on that
final luscious bite . . .
that's JUICY

When you're at Johnny Pemberton's crawfish boil and you
pop off a crawdad tail to suck that brothy nectar . . .
that's JUICY

When you're slammin' elote at Li'l Billy's b-day bash in
Elysian Park and get crema and cotija all over your face . . .
that's JUICY

When you're in Austin and you smear that brisket
in all the drippin's and barbecue sauce collected
on the butcher paper . . .
that's JUICY

When you're deep in Sicily and scoop that wildly fresh
bite of fish from the local olive oil and lemon juice
pooled on your plate . . .
that's JUICY

When you're in Oaxaca and buy the dankest of
dank moles from the market, dip that fresh warm
tortilla straight into the bag, and take a big-boy bite . . .
that's JUICY

naughty

NAUGHTY 'N' NICE GRILLED STEAKS

MAKES 2 SERVINGS

1 bone-in steak, such as porterhouse or rib-eye, about 3 inches thick

Kosher salt

Flaky sea salt (such as Maldon)

Extra-virgin olive oil and lemon wedges for serving "nice" style

Garlic Herb Butter (recipe follows) for serving "naughty" style

I love a big, gorgeous, fatty cut of beef cooked over a live fire, whether it's a tomahawk bone-in rib-eye or a dry-aged 2-pound porterhouse. Watching the flames lick the sides of the meat to form a smoky crust is a thing of pure beauty. Once this book hits shelves, I will have turned into a full fire freak, cooking EVERYTHING over dried oak and wearing one of those all-leather aprons, sporting a greasy mustache and a tattoo of a cow butchery chart on my tramp area.

First things first. Source your meat from a quality butcher. I love Cream Co. Meats, an incredible distributor based in Oakland that sells beef from sustainable or regenerative ranches direct to consumers. Ask your butcher what cuts they love to cook at home. Do they have any dry-aged pieces? Spend a few extra bucks to get a beautiful cut. Cooking on the bone helps the steak cook slower and more evenly, and offers a nice cushion so you don't accidentally overcook it. If you go past medium-rare, what are you even doing with your life? Treat this beautiful piece of meat with the respect it deserves and keep it juicy and red in the middle. Don't you dare trim off that fire-kissed fat. When rendered properly, that is the best part! Cut off a little piece and try it by itself. It's glorious.

When I'm feeling nice, I serve my steak simply, with a big splash of extra-virgin olive oil and maybe a green salad and braised beans on the side, like they do in Italy for bistecca alla fiorentina. But when I'm feeling like a li'l beef devil, I know I've got to serve it naughty style, with garlic herb butter slathered all over.

Pair the steak with something that can hold up to the richness. A 2016 Las Jaras Cab is fantastic. Or a Rhône red from Eric Texier. A Sangiovese from Podere le Boncie works perfectly, or you may want to splurge on a Montepulciano d'Abruzzo from Valentini or Emidio Pepe.

1 One or two hours before the steak is gonna hit the grill, pull it from the fridge. Season aggressively with kosher salt, making sure to hit the sides.

2 Prep your grill for two-zone cooking. If you're using charcoal, push the coals to one side so you have one super-hot zone for direct-heat cooking and a cooler zone for indirect cooking. If you're using gas, turn the heat up to high on one side and to medium-low on the other. Season the grates by rubbing plenty of oil all over with a paper towel. (Use tongs for this.) When your grill is screaming hot, put on the steak and sear both sides so they each have a nice, dark crust. If there's a fat cap, make sure to sear that too. Flare-ups are good here! Once you have nice caramelization, move the steak to the cooler zone, oriented so the bone is closest to the fire (this

helps shield and protect from overcooking), and cook until you reach an internal temperature of 120°F. Timing will vary depending on the thickness of your steak and heat of your grill—expect 3 to 4 minutes per side but use a meat thermometer to check.

3 Once the steak reaches 120°F, pull it from the heat and let it rest for 10 minutes before slicing. This rest time is essential. Respect the meat! Slice around the bone and then slice the steak against the grain. Sprinkle the carved steak with sea salt.

4 If you're feeling nice, pour a generous splash of olive oil over the top and serve with lemon wedges on the side. If you're feeling naughty, go for the French vibe and serve the steak topped with several pats of herb butter. Prepare yourself for a dankadent trip to Bonk Town.

If you have a food processor, puree the garlic and herbs, then add the butter and salt and pulse just until combined. Alternatively, finely mince the garlic and herbs and mash together with the butter and salt in a large bowl until well incorporated. Transfer the butter mixture to a sheet of plastic wrap, then mold into a cylinder and wrap completely. Store in the refrigerator until chilled, about 3 hours, or for up to 2 weeks.

GARLIC HERB BUTTER

MAKES ABOUT ½ CUP

1 garlic clove

2 tablespoons roughly chopped fresh herbs (such as tarragon, parsley, rosemary, or thyme)

½ cup unsalted butter, at room temperature

¼ teaspoon kosher salt

FILET AU POIVRE

MAKES 4 SERVINGS

Four 2-inch-thick filet mignons

Kosher salt

4½ tablespoons coarsely ground black pepper (see "Heimy's Hint," page 14)

2 tablespoons neutral oil

2 tablespoons minced shallots

¼ cup cognac or Calvados

¾ cup heavy cream

1½ tablespoons green peppercorns, drained

Steakhouse classics from the 1990s are underappreciated. Who doesn't love shrimp cocktail, tuna tartare, steak with a wedge salad and a martini on the side? Lately I've been doing steak au poivre with filet mignon, a cut that has a bit of a reputation for being played out. But I recently started buying really beautiful wagyu that has so much flavor, and it changed my whole perception.

More assertive cuts, like rib-eye, are beefy and intensely flavorful all on their own, so it would really be a crime to cover that flavor with a bunch of sauce. But because filet mignon is more of a neutral canvas, it's a great candidate for punchy sauces, like this au poivre. Steak au poivre (*poivre* is French for "pepper") is a French bistro classic. Madi's dad, Thomas Borbely, taught us this simple sauce. He's the incredible chef at Pizzas in the Mist in Robertson, Australia. He's on speed dial when Madi and I are cooking and need those real-deal chef tips. This recipe calls for green peppercorns, which are the unripe version of black peppercorns. They are typically preserved in brine and sold in little jars next to the capers.

Pair this with a bottle of New New from St. Reginald Parish. Their winemaker, Andy, makes a killer carbonic Pinot Noir.

1 About 30 minutes before you plan to cook the steaks, pull them from the fridge to come to room temperature. Season aggressively with salt, making sure to hit the sides. Preheat your oven to 350°F.

2 When you're ready to cook, pat the steaks dry with paper towels to wick away any excess moisture. Coat each steak with 1½ teaspoons of the black pepper, pressing to make sure the pepper really sticks.

3 In a large cast-iron skillet over high heat, warm the oil—you want this skillet screaming, around 500°F. Turn on your kitchen fans and open a window, because it's about to get smoky.

4 Add the steaks to the skillet and sear until the pepper forms a nice, dark bark, about 2 minutes per side, then transfer to the oven and cook for about 6 minutes, until an instant-read thermometer in the thickest part of the steak registers 120°F.

5 Remove the skillet from the oven and transfer the steaks to a cutting board to rest.

6 Place the skillet over medium heat, add the shallots to the cooking fat, and sauté until translucent, about 90 seconds. Add the cognac and deglaze the pan, using a wooden spoon to scrape up all the beefy bits from the bottom. Stir in the cream, green peppercorns, and remaining ½ tablespoon black pepper and lower the heat to maintain a low simmer. Cook, stirring, until the sauce has thickened and reduced slightly, about 5 minutes. You'll know it's done when it coats the back of your wooden spoon without running off. Season with salt.

7 Plate each filet mignon and drizzle the sauce over the tops before serving.

LAMB KABOBS
WITH GARLICKY TOMATOES

SERVES 4 TO 6

There were a few amazing Lebanese spots in Philadelphia that I loved to visit when I was growing up. That was when I was first introduced to the $2.50 falafel sandwich on a warm pita with silky hummus, tahini, and a splash of vinegary hot sauce—heaven. When I got older and started playing in punk bands, we would play at ABC No Rio on the Lower East Side of New York, and my first stop was always a falafel cart.

Moving to LA and hanging out in Glendale a lot introduced me to the wider world of Middle Eastern delicacies. At first we would spend every birthday and office party at Carousel, feasting on their fixed menu of kabobs, falafel, hummus, muhammara, and stuffed grape leaves. Go on Fridays for the belly dancing! These days, I have a much longer list of totally epic spots, but Skaf's, Akkad, and Mini Kabob are my favorites for freshness and flavor explosions.

For this dish, I got some help from the wonderful Armen Martirosyan, who, along with his parents, runs Mini Kabob in Glendale. It's a tiny, three-table Armenian Egyptian spot and one of my favorite restaurants ever. Armen and his folks take the time to grind their meat daily, resulting in the freshest, juiciest kabobs in town. Catch the Martirosyans in the right moment and you can hear them blasting spicy tunes and see Armen's mom and dad dancing in between their cooking duties.

I wanted to make a version of these gorgeous kabobs with ground lamb and do a slow-roasted tomato instead of a quick-cooked, blistered one, which is what they do at Mini Kabob. To get the timing right, start the tomatoes before you grill the kabobs. Pick up fresh lavash, an Armenian flatbread, and toum, an addictive garlicky sauce, at your local Middle Eastern grocery.

1 To make the kabobs: Line two baking sheets with parchment paper. Generously oil ten 10-inch-long metal skewers, or soak wooden skewers in a large bowl of water for 20 minutes.

2 In a large bowl, combine the lamb, egg, onion, garlic, tomato paste, mint, parsley, cumin, sumac, paprika, salt, and pepper and mix by hand just until incorporated. (Don't overmix or the meat will become tough.) Take a large handful (about ½ cup or 4½ ounces) of the meat mixture and shape it around a prepared skewer into an oblong sphere, about 8 inches long. Using your fingers, press down to flatten the sphere until it's a rectangle about 1 inch thick—this will help with more even grilling. As you shape each kabob, transfer it to a prepared baking sheet. Once all of the kabobs are formed, place them in the fridge for 30 minutes to firm up.

Kabobs

2 pounds ground lamb

1 egg

¼ yellow onion, very finely chopped

2 garlic cloves, finely minced

2 tablespoons tomato paste

2 tablespoons finely chopped mint

2 tablespoons finely chopped parsley

1 teaspoon ground cumin

1 teaspoon sumac

1 teaspoon smoked paprika

1 teaspoon kosher salt

1 teaspoon freshly ground black pepper

For Serving

Lavash

Lemon wedges

Pickled onions (see page 69)

Garlicky Tomatoes (recipe follows)

Tahini Spread (recipe follows)

Toum

continued

LAMB KABOBS,
CONTINUED

3 Prep your grill for direct, high-heat cooking—the target temperature is 500°F. Season the grates by rubbing plenty of oil all over with a paper towel. (Use tongs for this.) When your grill is hot and well oiled, add the kabobs and grill for about 4 minutes per side, flipping when the kabob starts to release itself from the grill grates. (You'll want tongs and a heat-proof spatula to flip the kabobs.)

4 To serve: Grill each piece of lavash just until warm, about 30 seconds per side.

5 Slide the meat off the skewers and arrange them on a serving plate with the flatbread, lemon wedges, pickled onions, and tomatoes. Pass bowls of tahini and toum on the side.

GARLICKY TOMATOES

MAKES ABOUT 2 CUPS

2 tablespoons extra-virgin olive oil

1 teaspoon kosher salt

½ teaspoon freshly ground black pepper

½ teaspoon ground cumin

½ teaspoon smoked paprika

½ teaspoon sumac

1 pound small tomatoes

4 garlic cloves, lightly crushed

1 handful chopped parsley

1 Preheat the grill to medium-high, about 300°F.

2 In a medium bowl, combine the olive oil, salt, pepper, cumin, paprika, and sumac and toss to combine. Add the tomatoes to the bowl and toss to coat, then transfer to a baking sheet. Set the baking sheet on the grill, close the lid, and cook for 20 minutes. Add the garlic to the baking sheet and cook for an additional 10 minutes, or until the tomatoes start to split. Remove from the heat and toss with the parsley before serving.

TAHINI SPREAD

MAKES ABOUT ½ CUP

¼ cup tahini

2 tablespoons lemon juice

¼ teaspoon kosher salt

¼ cup ice water

In a medium bowl, combine the tahini, lemon juice, and salt. Gradually drizzle in the ice water, whisking constantly, until your desired consistency is achieved. Store airtight in the fridge for up to 2 weeks.

SPICY SICHUAN RIB TICKLERS

MAKES 4 TO 6 SERVINGS

Alhambra in the San Gabriel Valley (SGV) is home to some of the best traditional Sichuan restaurants in the country and one of my fave spots to eat in the LA area. Bistro Na, I love you. Chef's Kiss! Over in NYC, Danny Bowien intro'd me to another level of Sichuan spice. I remember taking my first bite of one of his restaurant's signature dishes, Kung Pao Pastrami, and getting hit with this insane spicy-tingly sensation. I almost felt like I was high. It was so fucking good, an out-of-body experience.

Sichuan peppercorns aren't spicy—instead, they contribute an insane numbing sensation on your tongue. I've learned that the irresistible combination of spice and tingle is called *málà* in Mandarin Chinese, and that Sichuan peppercorns are a key player in many classic Sichuanese dishes.

While pork spareribs are a classic dish at many of the SGV restaurants that I love, this dish isn't traditional at all. Instead, I combined a lot of the ingredients from American barbecue sauce with more traditionally Chinese ingredients for a wild, spicy-tingly mash-up. I'm all about Herb Overload, especially on anything with a spicy glaze, which is why I cover these ribs with tons of fresh mint and cilantro and chopped peanuts at the end.

I tested this recipe dozens of times using various heat sources (smoker, grill, boiled on the stove top), but I prefer them wrapped in aluminum foil and roasted in the oven. You get such a juicy rib this way, almost fall-off-the-bone, but with a touch of structure. To drink, try it with a juicy red wine from the Jura. I love Julien Labet's reds; they have a magical tingle quality that matches the ribs.

This makes enough sauce and rub for two racks of ribs, but you can make just one rack if you have a smaller rib crew.

1 Preheat your oven to 250°F.

2 To make the dry rub: In a large mortar and using a pestle, combine the chiles, salt, and peppercorns and grind them into a coarse powder. Then individually add the fennel seeds, cloves, garlic powder, mustard powder, paprika, white pepper, cinnamon, and brown sugar and continue to grind until everything is incorporated. Alternatively, you can pulse the ingredients in a food processor.

3 Apply the dry rub evenly over the entire surface of each rack of ribs. Wrap each rack in aluminum foil two times, so the rib bones don't break the seal, and place on two baking sheets.

4 Bake until the meat is incredibly tender and begins to pull back from the bone a bit, about 2½ hours. When you poke the rib meat with a knife or fork, there should be very little resistance—that's how you know these ticklers are gonna melt in your mouth. If it ain't tender, keep cooking.

Dry Rub

2 dried Thai chiles, stemmed

2 tablespoons kosher salt

1 tablespoon Sichuan peppercorns

1 tablespoon fennel seeds

1 teaspoon whole cloves

1 tablespoon garlic powder

1 tablespoon mustard powder

1 tablespoon smoked paprika

1 tablespoon white pepper

1 teaspoon ground cinnamon

5 tablespoons packed brown sugar

2 racks pork spareribs

Tickle Sauce

1 cup packed brown sugar

1 cup ketchup

¼ cup rice wine vinegar

¼ cup Sriracha

3 tablespoons hoisin sauce

3 tablespoons soy sauce

2 tablespoons freshly grated ginger

2 tablespoons freshly grated garlic

1 tablespoon freshly ground Sichuan peppercorns (see "Heimy's Hint," page 14)

1 tablespoon kosher salt

1 tablespoon white pepper

½ cup chopped peanuts

½ cup chopped mint

½ cup chopped cilantro

continued

5 To make the tickle sauce: While the ribs are cooking, in a medium saucepan over medium-high heat, stir together the brown sugar, ketchup, vinegar, Sriracha, hoisin, soy sauce, ginger, garlic, ground peppercorns, salt, and white pepper and bring to a boil. Once the sauce is boiling, lower the heat so that the sauce just barely simmers and cook, stirring occasionally, until reduced by half, about 30 minutes.

6 Once the ribs have reached doneness, unwrap the foil, taking care to preserve all of the beautiful drippings and cooking juices that have accumulated. Add 1 cup of the drippings (or however much there is, if it's less than 1 cup) to the sauce.

7 Turn the oven temperature to 400°F. Cover a baking sheet in aluminum foil and set a wire rack on top.

8 Place the unwrapped ribs on the prepared rack and, using a pastry brush, coat the entire surface of the ribs evenly with the sauce. Bake for 15 minutes, then baste the ribs again with the sauce.

9 Turn on the broiler and broil, watching very carefully, until the ribs look freaking magical, with plenty of charred, caramelized spots on the surface, about 5 minutes.

10 Transfer the ribs to a cutting board or serving platter, slice between the bones, and sprinkle with the chopped peanuts, mint, and cilantro. Serve immediately.

SPICE ON MY LIPS
SPICE ON MY HIPS

SAUSAGE
WITH TUSCAN BEANS

MAKES 2 SERVINGS

¼ cup extra-virgin olive oil, plus more for drizzling

2 mild Italian pork sausages

5 garlic cloves; 4 thinly sliced, 1 smashed

1 large tomato, diced

Kosher salt

1½ teaspoons red pepper flakes

5 sprigs rosemary; 3 cut into thirds

Freshly ground black pepper

One 15-ounce can cannellini beans with their liquid

One 2-inch piece Pecorino Romano rind, plus 1 tablespoon finely grated Pecorino Romano

1 tablespoon lemon juice

Two 1-inch slices crusty bread

Beautiful white beans and fresh pork sausage are a match made in Italian heaven. If you cook the Heimy way, you will always have nice, big pieces of Parmigiano-Reggiano and Pecorino Romano cheese in your fridge. Save your rinds. You can toss them into soups and stews (and in this case, beans) to add an incredible umami note.

1 In a deep sauté pan over medium heat, warm 1 tablespoon of the olive oil. Add the sausages and cook until browned on all sides, 5 to 7 minutes. Transfer the sausages to a plate and set aside.

2 Turn the heat to low and add the sliced garlic to the pan. Sauté until soft and fragrant, 1 to 2 minutes—you're looking to soften the garlic, not brown it. Turn the heat to medium; add 2 tablespoons olive oil, the tomato, 1½ teaspoons salt, red pepper flakes, half of the cut rosemary, and five cranks of black pepper; and stir to combine. Once the mixture begins to bubble, turn the heat to medium-low and simmer gently until the tomato begins to break down, about 3 minutes.

3 Drain half of the liquid from the beans, then add the beans and the remaining liquid to the tomato mixture. Simmer until the sauce is well integrated and slightly reduced, about 5 minutes.

4 Return the sausages to the pan and add the Pecorino rind and remaining 1 tablespoon olive oil. Cover the pan and let simmer until the sausages are cooked through, 12 to 15 minutes. (To test doneness, prick the sausages with a fork. They are done when the juices run clear.) Stir in the remaining cut rosemary and the lemon juice and remove from the heat.

5 Meanwhile, generously drizzle both sides of each piece of bread with olive oil. In a skillet over medium heat, fry the bread until each side is golden and toasted. Remove from the pan and rub the smashed garlic on each side and sprinkle with the grated Pecorino. Cut each slice of bread into thirds.

6 Divide the bean and tomato mixture among two bowls and nestle a sausage into each. Finish with a liberal drizzle of olive oil, a sprig of rosemary, and slices of toasted bread before serving.

WHOLE FISH WRAPPED IN FIG LEAVES
WITH SALSA VERDE

MAKES 4 SERVINGS

During the Great QUAR of 2020, my buddy Chris Kronner started selling insanely high-quality fish and shellfish in the LA area. He was like a seafood Santa Claus delivering ocean goodies right to your door. He turned me on to this fig leaf–wrapped whole fish, which blew my mind. The fig leaves help the fish steam while infusing the flesh with this subtle leaf flavor. Up to that point, I'd always done my whole fish right on the grill. That gives you a lovely, crispy charred skin, so if you don't have access to fig leaves, you can oil your grates really well and grill the fish without the wrapping.

But if you wanna go to the next level of flavor and moistness, and you have friends or neighbors with fig trees in their yard, sneak off in the night and snip off a few leaves to use here.

Once again, the key is to make friends with your fishmonger. Ask what's the best fish they have whole for grilling. Branzino is always a safe bet and a super-delicious fish! I've had many a whole branzino in Greece and Italy. Fishmongers will clean it for you, so all you need to do is stuff it with aromatics. Paired with a crisp, cold white wine and seasoned simply with herbs and lemon, this is one of my fave fish experiences ever.

1 To make the salsa verde: An hour before you plan to grill (this gives your flavors time to infuse), in a mortar, and using a pestle, combine the parsley, capers, garlic, anchovy, and 2 teaspoons salt and crush into a rough paste. Add the lemon juice and stir to combine, then slowly drizzle in the olive oil and whisk until you have a well-integrated emulsion. (If you don't have a mortar and pestle, chop the parsley, capers, garlic, anchovy, and salt into as fine a paste as possible, occasionally smashing the mixture with the flat of your knife. Then transfer it to a bowl, stir in the lemon juice, and drizzle in the olive oil.) Taste and season with more salt or lemon juice as needed. Set aside.

2 Season each fish generously with salt and pepper, making sure to get inside the cavity as well. Layer two-thirds of the lemon slices and the herb sprigs inside the cavities.

Salsa Verde

1 cup chopped flat-leaf parsley

2 tablespoons capers, drained

2 garlic cloves, smashed

1 anchovy fillet

Kosher salt

3 tablespoons lemon juice, or as needed

5 tablespoons extra-virgin olive oil

Two 1½-pound whole fish (such as branzino), gutted and cleaned

Kosher salt and freshly ground black pepper

3 lemons, thinly sliced and seeded

3 or 4 sprigs flat-leaf parsley, plus leaves for sprinkling

3 or 4 sprigs tarragon, plus leaves for sprinkling

3 or 4 sprigs thyme, plus leaves for sprinkling

8 to 16 fig leaves, washed well and tough stems removed, as needed

Extra-virgin olive oil for drizzling

continued

3 Arrange some of the fig leaves on your work surface, overlapping them to form an oval that's wide enough to enclose the body of a fish. Drizzle olive oil on the fig leaves where you plan to place the fish, then lay the fish on top and drizzle more oil on top of that. Wrap the leaves so that the body of the fish is completely covered (you can leave the head and tail exposed), then use butcher's twine to secure the fig leaves in place. Repeat with the remaining fig leaves and fish.

4 Prepare your grill for indirect cooking over medium-high heat. Season the grates by rubbing plenty of neutral oil all over with a paper towel. (Use tongs for this.)

5 Place the fig leaf–wrapped fish on the grates and grill for 6 minutes, then, using tongs and a spatula, gently flip the fish and cook on the other side for 6 minutes more. At this point, peek under the fig leaves and check the fish for doneness: the flesh should be opaque and flaky. If it is still translucent, continue cooking.

6 Serve the fish with the remaining lemon slices on the side. Remove the twine and peel back the fig leaves and skin to reveal the tender flesh, then drizzle with the salsa verde and sprinkle with herb leaves.

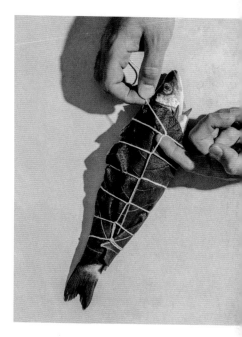

CEVICHE
WITH LECHE DE TIGRE

MAKES 4 SERVINGS

1 pound halibut or other fresh whitefish, cut into ½-inch pieces

Kosher salt

Leche de Tigre

1 cup lime juice

½ fresh aji amarillo or Fresno chile

¼ cup chopped celery hearts (the tender white interior part)

¼ cup chopped red onion

¼ cup chopped cilantro stems

3 garlic cloves

2 tablespoons diced ginger

2 tablespoons fish scraps

1 tablespoon sugar, plus more as needed

Kosher salt

4 ice cubes

1 small orange sweet potato or yam, peeled

½ cup cancha or Corn Nuts

1 teaspoon neutral oil

Kosher salt

½ small red onion, sliced as thin as possible, soaked in water to cover for 5 minutes, and patted dry

½ fresh aji amarillo or Fresno chile, stemmed but not seeded and thinly sliced

Roughly chopped cilantro for garnish

I was turned on to this dish at Sabor a Peru, a fantastic restaurant in Miami where I had my first shot of Tiger's Milk—the name for the spicy, citrusy liquid used in Peruvian cooking to marinate ceviche. There, they serve the leche in a shot glass alongside the ceviche—when I knocked it back, I was hit with a rush of energy. I was hooked. (I later learned that leche de tigre is said to be an aphrodisiac and hangover cure—bonus!)

J.D. Plotnick, one of my wine mentors and a former chef who spent a lot of time in Peru, helped me crack the code to this perfect dish. You'll want to buy cancha—also known as maiz chulpe—at a Latin market or online. It's an amazing Peruvian snack made from corn kernels that you fry up— they puff and soften, putting them somewhere between Corn Nuts and popcorn. Corn Nuts will work in a pinch as a substitute. Aji amarillo is an orange pepper you can find jarred in groceries with Peruvian specialties. If you can't find it, you can sub a spicy red chile, like jalapeño or Fresno.

1. Season the fish with salt and place in the refrigerator.

2. To make the leche de tigre: In a food processor or blender, combine the lime juice, chile, celery hearts, chopped onion, cilantro, garlic, ginger, fish scraps, sugar, ½ teaspoon salt, and ice cubes and puree to incorporate. Taste and adjust the seasoning with more sugar or salt as needed. It should be very zingy but also balanced. Strain through a fine-mesh strainer to remove all the solids and transfer to the refrigerator.

3. Place the sweet potato in a medium pot of salted water and bring to a boil.

4. Meanwhile, fill a large bowl with ice cubes and water to prepare an ice bath.

5. Cook the potato until fork-tender, 25 to 35 minutes, depending on its size. Immediately transfer to the ice bath. Once cooled, slice the potato into ¼-inch-thick pieces.

6. In a medium saucepan, combine the cancha and oil, cover the pan, and place over medium heat. Cook, shaking frequently, until you hear the kernels pop—it will sound like popcorn but the kernels won't burst open. This should take about 4 minutes. Remove from the heat, then drain and season with salt.

7. Fill a large bowl with ice, then place a mixing bowl on top of the ice. Make sure to save a shot glass of leche de tigre for everyone! Add the remaining leche de tigre to the mixing bowl, then the raw fish and toss to combine. Let sit until the fish reaches your desired doneness, 10 to 15 minutes. As the citrus gently cooks the fish, the flesh will start to turn opaque, but the interior should still be raw.

8. Divide the ceviche among four serving bowls, garnish with the sweet potato, cancha, sliced red onion, chile, and cilantro, then serve immediately. Now's the time to bring out those shots of leche, for your health.

CAPERED CRUDO

MAKES 4 SERVINGS

This crudo takes me back to Sicily, where I visited Taverna la Cialoma in Marzamemi, a terrace restaurant that overlooks the insanely blue waters of the Ionian Sea at the southernmost tip of the island. There, we ate the freshest raw fish and shrimp, seasoned super-simply with capers, olive oil, and citrus. Talk to your fishmonger and let them recommend the best sushi-grade fish for the dish.

1 tablespoon extra-virgin olive oil

1 tablespoon capers, drained

6 ounces sashimi-grade fish (such as tuna, fluke, halibut, or cod), trimmed and sliced ¼ inch thick

High-quality extra-virgin olive oil for drizzling

Flaky sea salt (such as Maldon)

½ lemon

1 Put a serving plate in the fridge to chill. Line another plate with a double layer of paper towels.

2 In a small, cold saucepan, combine the olive oil and capers. Set over medium-low heat and sauté until the capers are crispy and fragrant, 2 to 3 minutes. Transfer the capers to the prepared plate to drain and cool.

3 Arrange the fish on the chilled serving plate. Generously drizzle high-quality extra-virgin olive oil over the top and season with sea salt, then squeeze lemon juice over each piece. Evenly distribute the capers, then grate the zest of the lemon over all. Serve immediately.

YUM YUM

GRAPEFRUIT SASHIMI

MAKES 4 SERVINGS

4 ounces sashimi-grade hamachi, or another delicate fish, sliced ⅛ inch thick

2 small, sweet grapefruits (such as Rio Star or Ruby Sweet), supremed (see Note)

Up to 1 tablespoon lemon juice

1 tablespoon ponzu

½ tablespoon soy sauce, or to taste

⅛ teaspoon finely grated ginger

Extra-virgin olive oil for drizzling

Cilantro leaves or cilantro flowers, torn into small pieces, for garnish

This dish is an homage to all the incredible Japanese-inspired joints that are around in LA. I'm a sucker for a Nobu-style sashimi plate with fresh fruit.

1 On a serving plate, fan alternating slices of hamachi and grapefruit attractively to form a sort of pinwheel pattern. (If any of the supremes are much thicker than the hamachi slices, cut them in half lengthwise so they're roughly the same thickness.)

2 In a small bowl, combine any accumulated grapefruit juice from the supreming with as much lemon juice as needed to reach 1 tablespoon. Add the ponzu, soy sauce, and ginger and stir to incorporate. Taste and adjust the seasoning if needed (if you like it a little saltier, add some more soy. If your citrus is super-sour and you feel like the sauce needs to be sweeter, you can stir in the tiniest pinch of sugar).

3 Drizzle the citrus-soy sauce gingerly over the fish and grapefruit—you may not use all of it, so go slow. Then, drizzle a bit of extra-virgin olive oil over the top of everything and garnish with the cilantro. Serve immediately.

Note: *Supreming* is a fancy term for segmenting grapefruits so you remove all of the flesh but leave behind the bitter pith and membrane. First, peel the grapefruit with a knife, cutting off the top and bottom, then cut away all the peel and pith from the sides of the grapefruit in large strips. Now it's time to "supreme"—hold the fruit over a bowl to catch all the tasty juice. Using a paring knife, slice along one edge of a segment, separating the flesh from the membrane, until you get to the center. Repeat on the other edge of the segment—a tasty grapefruit wedge should pop out. Repeat with the remaining grapefruit segments.

CLAMS AND MUSSELS IN SPICE BROTH

WITH GARLIC DIPPERS

MAKES 4 SERVINGS

2 pounds clams

2 pounds mussels

2 tablespoons extra-virgin olive oil

1 tablespoon unsalted butter

1 cup diced yellow onion

1 cup thinly sliced fennel

8 garlic cloves, minced

2 teaspoons Calabrian chili paste (or more, if you like it hot)

2 teaspoons kosher salt

2 teaspoons freshly ground black pepper

1 cup white wine

1 cup whole canned tomatoes, crushed by hand

Juice of 2 lemons

Garlic Dippers

1 rustic sourdough loaf, sliced ½ inch thick and cut into strips

Extra-virgin olive oil for drizzling

1 garlic head with the top fourth removed

Chopped flat-leaf parsley for garnish

In so many seaside towns in Italy, they do this beautiful tomato-and-fennel-y seafood stew, with whatever fresh shellfish they've hauled in that day. The preparation is so briny and flavorful, and I always assumed it was really complicated to make. It's not, though! Turns out cooking clams and mussels at home is super-easy; you always know when they're cooked properly because that's the minute they pop open. Boom!

The best part about this dish is the spicy, salty broth, which tastes and smells like the sea. I was born to dip, so you know I'm gonna plunge some fragrant garlic dippers into that tasty sauce.

❶ Scrub clean the clams and mussels. Purge the clams by placing them in a bowl filled with cold water for 15 minutes to release any sand, then drain. Discard any clams or mussels that are not closed.

❷ In a Dutch oven or a pot large enough to fit all the shellfish, combine the olive oil and butter and set over medium heat. Add the onion and fennel and sauté until soft and the onion is translucent, about 5 minutes. Add the garlic, chili paste, salt, and pepper and cook just until fragrant, 1 to 2 minutes more. Add the wine and deglaze the pan, using a wooden spoon to scrape up any of the tasty, crusty bits stuck to the bottom. Cook until you can't smell the alcohol anymore, about 5 minutes. Add the tomatoes and lemon juice and bring to a simmer. Cook, stirring occasionally, until the flavors meld, about 5 minutes. Taste and adjust the seasoning as needed.

❸ Add the clams and mussels to the broth, stir to combine, cover the pot, and cook until all the mussels and clams have opened, about 5 minutes. (If any refuse to open up, they've probably gone bad—throw them away.)

❹ To make the garlic dippers: Preheat your broiler and arrange the bread on a baking sheet. Drizzle both sides of the bread with olive oil and place the baking sheet on the middle rack. Broil, watching carefully, until the bread is super-toasty, about 2 minutes per side. (I like it almost burnt. The sauce will rehydrate the bread, so you get this magical texture combo.) As soon as you pull the toast from the oven, rub the exposed flesh of the garlic head all over both sides of the bread.

❺ Divide the mussels and clams and their broth among four bowls. Garnish with parsley and serve with the dippers to get all the tasty, spicy broth.

RACLETTE PARTY

In the European Alps, they've taken the act of melting cheese and elevated it into an art form. Everyone knows fondue, the regional specialty of the Swiss Alps and 1970s dinner parties. Less familiar might be the tradition of raclette, which is a specific type of semihard cheese that is popular in Switzerland and the Savoie region of eastern France. There, they slowly melt a giant wheel of cheese in front of a live fire, allowing the molten runoff to land atop a plate of potatoes and charcuterie.

One of the best gifts I've ever received is a raclette grill, which you can buy online or at any kitchenware store. It comes with eight individual cheese paddles so that you can melt your own cheese under the electric heating element, plus a cooktop on which you can sizzle up meats and veg. Individual cheese paddles, DIY meat sizzling? This is next-level cheese action. It's also just an incredibly fun style of communal dining. Everyone gets the satisfaction of personally grilling their own meats—which is particularly great for people who maybe aren't experienced cooks and have never had the pleasure of grilling their own steak.

My good friend Nic Harvard, who was the first assistant director of *Tim & Eric's Billion Dollar Movie*, introduced me to his mom, who is French and a fancy caterer to the stars. She told me the true secret of raclette: You're not allowed to drink any water when you're eating it. Only wine, or a bit of schnapps. If you drink water, she said, your tummy will block up with all the congealed cheese.

My Heimy-fied twist on that tradition is to end a Raclette Party with mini-bottles of Underberg, a bracing, incredibly bitter German liqueur. When everyone is feeling full to the point of bursting, I don my Underberg bandolier and walk around the party, dispensing restorative bottles of bitter to my beleaguered guests.

MENU AND SHOPPING LIST

Cheese: Raclette is the traditional choice here.

Salads, for crunch and brightness: Opa Salad (page 206) and Tomaten Salad (page 208).

Fruit and pickle plates, to help cut through the fat: Cornichons, pickled onions, caperberries, fresh kumquats, or tart grapes.

Meats: High-quality beef, sliced thin. Skirt steak works great, or you can slice a boneless rib-eye or sirloin about ¼ inch thick. The more fat marbling, the better. Also buy some nice charcuterie; for example, saucisson sec (a French-style salami typically made with pork; slice it ⅛ inch thick), brési (Swiss cured beef; buy it sliced), or jambon (French or Swiss ham; buy it sliced).

Bread: Sliced baguette or pain au levain.

Vegetables, for grilling: Potatoes, boiled in salted water until tender and cut into bite-size pieces. Meaty mushrooms such as king oyster mushrooms, chanterelles, or other wild mushrooms, sliced ¼ inch thick.

Cheese wines: See page 194.

CHEESE WINES

Whenever possible, I try to pair specific regional dishes with wines that also come from the area. So, the obvious match for the Alpine dishes of a raclette party are Alpine wines, like the crisp, minerally whites from the Savoie in France. Another good bet is wines from the Jura, also in eastern France, a mountainous region where iconic Comté cheese is made. (The Jura also happens to be where I took my first wine trip.) I tend to lean heavily on white wines here, since the brightness and acidity help to cut through the fat. But keep a few bottles of juicy, lighter-body reds on hand too.

If you're having friends bring bevs, ask them to look for mountain wines that go well with hearty, fatty, cheesy goodness—any good wine store should be able to point them in the right direction. Here are some of my favorites.

- Sparkling whites from Domaine Belluard (region: Savoie; grape: local varieties, like Gringet and Altesse). Look for his "Les Alpes" bottling.

- Chardonnay from Jean-François Ganevat (region: Jura; grape: Chardonnay, although his Savagnin wines are amazing too).

- Nice German Riesling (region: Germany; grape: Riesling). Don't be afraid to go with an off-dry Riesling here; a little sweetness makes sense with the cheeses!

- Mondeuse or another red wine from Jean-Yves Péron (region: Savoie; grape: Mondeuse).

- Italian Alpine reds, like those from Les Crêtes (region: Valle d'Aosta; grapes: Nebbiolo, local varieties like Petit Rouge).

- Fancy red Burgundy (region: Burgundy; grape: Pinot Noir). No, it's not a mountain wine, but I can't resist any opportunity to pull out a beautiful Burgundy from Simon Bize.

HOW TO DO IT

1 Find a nice cheese shop. If they don't have the specific cheese that I've recommended, tell them you're hosting a raclette party and need some meltable cheese, preferably from the Swiss or French Alps.

2 Make the salads (wait to dress them until later) and arrange your fruit and pickle plates.

3 Assemble bonkers cold-cut and cheese boards; allow to come to room temperature.

4 Slice some bread, boil the potatoes, and prep veggies and additional meats for raclette.

5 Set up the raclette grill and bring everything to the table. Dress your salads.

6 Go full-on bliss mode as you pour molten cheese over everything.

7 Take breaks! Walk around the block. Stare at the stars and give your friend a hug. Then come home for more cheese.

8 Give thanks for all the wines that enable you to eat even more cheese.

GREEN FOODS

Beige is beautiful, but eating green is a dream. Life is a spectrum of color and emotions; and a lot of the time, I'm in a green mood. Green is GOOD. Green is Mother Earth. Green is a perfect snap pea. Turns out your Mem Mem was right and you MUST get your greens in if you want to transcend to Heimy Level.

When done right, gorgeous greens are something that I CRAVE. For example, the Opa Salad on page 206 is crisp, is high-acid, and highlights beautiful green butter lettuce, rather than smothering its flavor with too much dressing. You can apply this to all veggies. Get your sauces and dressings on point, make sure they highlight rather than hide your veg, and you'll elevate your cooking. I also crave a perfect crudité spread as much as a rib roast at times. I was a vegetarian for many years and, because I love my veggie chippies, I have thrown in a couple of meat-free main dishes at the end of the chapter. For your health!

CRUDITÉ EXTREME
WITH DILL DIPPER

MAKES 4 TO 6 SERVINGS

Dill Dipper

1 cup Greek yogurt

¼ cup milk

¼ cup chopped flat-leaf parsley

1 tablespoon fresh lemon juice

1 tablespoon extra-virgin olive oil

1 teaspoon chopped dill

1 teaspoon sumac

½ teaspoon kosher salt

½ teaspoon freshly ground black pepper

1 tablespoon thinly sliced green onion (green parts)

Rosemary-Chile Oil (page 67) for drizzling (optional)

Fresh, in-season vegetables, cleaned and trimmed (see Note)

Many years ago, I was invited to the housewarming party of a certain '90s-era goth-industrial musician known for his white face makeup, dark eyeliner and lipstick, and crazy on-stage antics. He had just moved from his Hollywood apartment to a more refined mansion in the hills—it had a very ornate, medieval vibe.

I was hoping for blood cocktails and live fires with hunks of lamb spinning on human-bone spits; but when I walked inside, I noticed that there were only three plastic trays of crusty precut veggies from the local grocery chain. Some of them were still shrink-wrapped, with the plastic just barely peeled back. I couldn't resist going up to my host and hassling him a bit—"Dude, you have this giant beautiful house. You're an adult now. What's with the plastic veg?!" His mood changed, then he turned to whisper something to one of the staff members working the party. Next thing I knew, the veg trays were quickly whisked away and tossed into the side yard!

My number-one hosting tip is you should always have a nice crudité plate with dippers waiting for your guests when they arrive. Buy primo, in-season produce and take the time to peel and trim all the vegetables yourself. Don't you dare look at the pre-trimmed crudité trays sold in grocery stores. Arrange your cut vegetables attractively on a nice plate.

1 To make the dipper: In a serving bowl, combine the yogurt, milk, parsley, lemon juice, olive oil, dill, sumac, salt, and pepper and stir to combine. Sprinkle with the green onions and attractively drizzle a swirl of chile oil, if desired, on top.

2 Arrange all the vegetables on a platter and serve alongside your beautiful, delicious dipper.

Note: I'm not really a fan of crudité plates where all the vegetables are trimmed into identical matchstick shapes. Instead, try to just peel and trim the vegetables into more bite-friendly versions of their natural shape. This is easier to do if you buy smaller, "baby" versions of vegetables, like carrots or fennel, which you can serve whole or cut vertically into wedges.

Some ideas for vegetables to use are radishes, snap peas, and baby carrots in spring; cherry tomatoes, squash, quickly blanched green beans, cucumbers and bell peppers in summer; endive (cut in half), small lettuces (either cut in half vertically or separated into leaves), and fennel in the fall and winter.

RAYS OF HEAVEN

MAKES 4 SERVINGS

1 large yellow heirloom
tomato

2 yellow peaches

2 figs

¼ cup roasted hazelnuts, very
roughly chopped (mostly half
and whole pieces)

High-quality aged balsamic
vinegar for drizzling

Extra-virgin olive oil
for drizzling

Flaky smoked sea salt
(such as Maldon)

Small leaves of basil or
basil flowers (look for 'em
at the farmers' market) for
sprinkling

If it isn't the height of summer when you're reading this, put this book down, go back to bed, pull the covers over your head, and pray to Jangus that the seasons will change quickly so you can FULLY enjoy this miracle of a dish. The key to the recipe is ripeness—you need to find the best fruit and veg at the peak of their season. In Los Angeles, we have about a month of insanely sweet peaches, and I go hog wild at the farmers' market. Dress this salad lightly to play off the natural sweetness of the fruit. I have a bright, lemony olive oil that is perfect with this. I love it when the hazelnuts are still slightly warm, and the peaches, tomato, and figs are room temp.

1 Cut the tomato and peaches into equal-size wedges. Cut the figs into smaller wedges.

2 Arrange the veg and fruit circularly on a serving plate. (I like to start by fanning the figs in a small circle in the center of the plate, then alternate wedges of tomato and peach in a concentric circle around the outside.) Sprinkle with the hazelnuts, then finish with light drizzles of balsamic and olive oil. Sprinkle with the sea salt and basil before serving.

MEAT SALAD

MAKES 4 SERVINGS

The combination of prosciutto and cantaloupe is one of the all-time great Mediterranean pairings. It's a summertime classic, and you can find it all over Italy and southern France. As always, the key is to buy perfect prosciutto and to pick out the ripest melon. Lots of people have tricks for picking the best melon in the store, but to be honest, the best way is to just give it a whiff. If you can smell fragrant melon-y goodness through the rind, then it's good to go. If you don't smell anything, say nish and move on to the next one.

At Shibucho, an amazing sushi restaurant in Los Angeles, the chef let me in on a li'l melon secret. When I asked him about the green melon he had served me—it tasted like the wildly expensive but incredibly flavorful musk melons you can get in Japan—he told me his trick is to buy melons almost ripe and then let them sit in the trunk of his car for two days. The heat reduces and strengthens the sugars in those dream spheres. We replicated this technique at my friend Bryan Hollon's wedding in Tuscany, when the melons we found at the market were subpar. After two days sitting in the helmet storage boxes on our scooters, they were gold!

Get yourself a nice serving platter and have fun with the plating. I usually arrange the melons first, drape pieces of prosciutto on top, then go for figs and everything else. The pickled chiles add a nice pop to cut through the deliciously decadent ham.

1 small ripe melon (such as cantaloupe), or ½ of a larger melon, peeled, cored, and cut into long wedges

10 slices prosciutto, cut very thin

4 figs, halved

1 handful shelled pistachios

1 handful basil leaves

Pickled serrano or Fresno chiles (see page 69) for serving

Extra-virgin olive oil for drizzling

Flaky smoked sea salt (such as Maldon)

Arrange the melon on a serving plate and drape the prosciutto over the top. Place the figs on the serving plate, then sprinkle the pistachios, basil, and chiles over everything. Drizzle with olive oil and season with a pinch of sea salt. Serve immediately.

OPA SALAD

MAKES 4 SERVINGS

¼ cup apple cider vinegar

2 teaspoons sugar

1 teaspoon kosher salt

2 tablespoons minced shallots

2 tablespoons extra-virgin olive oil

1 head butter lettuce, separated into leaves

1 handful fresh herbs (such as tarragon, parsley, oregano, or marjoram), roughly chopped

Growing up, we used to visit my oma and opa in Offenau, Germany. They had this tiny little yard, and every inch of it was covered with their kitchen garden. They grew redcurrants and gooseberries, which they turned into jams and beautiful cakes, and tomatoes and lettuces that they made into salads.

I still have very vivid memories of watching my opa go out and clip greens and herbs to make a simple salad. The best part was that the veg would still be a bit warm from the sun—that's how fresh this salad was. Every time I make this salad I think of him (and also how he hated American Hershey's chocolate).

1 In a small bowl, whisk together the vinegar, sugar, and salt. Add the shallots and allow to marinate for 15 minutes, so the shallots lose a bit of their bite. Gradually whisk in the olive oil until emulsified into a dressing.

2 Wash and dry the lettuce, place in a large bowl, and then add the herbs and dressing. Toss gently with your hands so that each leaf is covered. Serve immediately.

CHEF'S KISS

TOMATEN SALAD

MAKES 4 SERVINGS

¼ cup red wine vinegar

2 teaspoons sugar (optional; omit if your vinegar is already sweet)

1 teaspoon kosher salt

2 tablespoons minced shallots

1 tablespoon extra-virgin olive oil

1½ pounds heirloom tomatoes, cut into bite-size pieces

1 handful fresh parsley leaves, roughly chopped

My mom is a big gardener, just like my oma and opa. She moved to Baltimore from Germany in the early 1970s and was shocked by how bad the grocery-store produce sections in the United States were. Between that and the fact that we didn't have a lot of money, she preferred growing her own food—it was in her DNA. So, we always had a massive garden while growing up, and my mom was especially proud of her tomatoes.

I didn't quite appreciate how lucky I was until I got older and began to realize that in-season produce grown with care by farmers you know is always going to taste better than the generic, mass-farmed stuff that gets trucked in from who-knows-where.

Because of my family, I always assumed that this love for farm-fresh produce was a German thing, but then I traveled all over the world and tasted the incredible vegetables in so many of the countries I visited, and I realized that it really is universal. This salad, though, is a nod to my German heritage (and a direct descendant of the Opa Salad on page 206) and a thank-you to my mom for showing me the beauty of ripe, homegrown tomatoes. Danke, Mutti!

1 In a small bowl, whisk together the vinegar, sugar (if using), and salt. Add the shallots and allow to marinate for 15 minutes, so the shallots lose a bit of their bite. Gradually whisk in the olive oil until emulsified into a dressing.

2 In a large bowl, combine the tomatoes and parsley, add the dressing, and toss gently. Serve immediately.

FAVAS, SHAVED FENNEL, AND PARMIGIANO-REGGIANO

MAKES 4 SERVINGS

Favas are cool. They look like giant pea pods; and when they're in season in late spring and early summer, I simply cannot resist. They take a bit of work to prepare—first you have to shell the favas, then you have to boil them and remove the tough outer skin from each individual bean—but I think it's worth it for that creamy, pea-like taste. It feels good to use your hands, and putting in a bit of effort makes this salad taste even more delicious and soulful. Put on some of your favorite tunes, turn off your phone, and get into the Fava Experience.

3 pounds fresh fava beans

1 small bulb fennel, trimmed

1 handful fresh mint, large leaves torn

2 ounces shaved Parmigiano-Reggiano, plus more for serving

Extra-virgin olive oil for drizzling

1 lemon

Kosher salt and freshly ground black pepper

1 Shell the favas to remove the beans from their pods. Then bring a large pot of salted water to a boil and fill a large bowl with ice cubes and water to prepare an ice bath.

2 Add the favas to the boiling water and cook until tender and the beans easily slip out of their skins—this should take between 2 and 5 minutes, depending on the size of the favas. You can test for doneness by gently squeezing one of the beans and seeing if it pops out of its little casing. As soon as the favas are tender, transfer them to the ice bath to cool. Then, pop all of the beans out of their skins and transfer them to a serving bowl.

3 Shave the fennel as thinly as possible (a mandoline works best for this) and add to the favas. Add the mint and Parm and drizzle everything with olive oil. Squeeze half of the lemon over the top, add a pinch each of salt and pepper, and toss to coat. Taste and adjust the seasoning, adding more lemon, salt, or pepper as needed. Finish with long shaved pieces of Parm and another drizzle of olive oil. Serve at room temperature.

TOASTED BREAD SALAD

MAKES 4 SERVINGS

2 cups 1-inch-cubed ciabatta

Extra-virgin olive oil for drizzling, plus ¼ cup

Kosher salt

3 tablespoons Moscato vinegar

¼ teaspoon Dijon mustard

1 garlic clove, finely grated

Freshly ground black pepper

1 cup 1-inch-diced tomatoes

¼ cup green olives

1 cucumber, peeled, seeded, and cut on the bias into 1-inch pieces

2 tablespoons thinly sliced red onion

1 handful basil
(large leaves torn)

1 handful flat-leaf parsley leaves

1 pinch fresh oregano

In Italy, salad made from stale bread scraps softened in olive oil and tomato juices is called panzanella. My tip is to cut the bread, cucumbers, and tomatoes into similar-size pieces so that the salad looks adorable and each bite is balanced. Sweetness in your vinegar is key here. If you don't have Moscato vinegar, you may need to add ½ teaspoon of sugar to the vinaigrette to compensate.

I like ciabatta for its airiness and perfect flavor. Sourdough is a li'l too heavy for this dish; but really, any bread scraps will do in a pinch.

My fave panzanella memory is eating a crispy salad at Marigold restaurant in Rome in the middle of summer. Nothing compares to that perfect produce, which balanced out all of my cacio e pepe consumption.

Chloe Wise's salad art has inspired my cooking for many years. The painting at right is her interpretation of Toasted Bread Salad.

1 Preheat your oven to 400°F.

2 Place the ciabatta on a rimmed baking sheet and toss with a drizzle of olive oil and a pinch of salt. Bake until toasted, about 6 minutes. Set aside.

3 In a medium bowl, combine the vinegar, mustard, and garlic and whisk to incorporate. Gradually drizzle in the ¼ cup olive oil, whisking continuously until emulsified into a vinaigrette. Season with ½ teaspoon salt and ¼ teaspoon pepper. Add 1 tablespoon of the vinaigrette to the tomatoes and let sit for 5 minutes to macerate.

4 Smash the olives with the flat part of your knife, then remove the pits.

5 In a large bowl, combine the toasted bread, tomatoes and their liquid, olives, cucumber, onion, basil, and parsley and stir to incorporate. Season with additional salt, pepper, and as much of the remaining vinaigrette as desired. Top with the oregano. Serve with a slotted spoon so that the salad doesn't puddle too much on your serving plate, then enjoy immediately, while the bread is still a li'l warm.

GREEN GLOBE CURRY

MAKES 4 SERVINGS

1 tablespoon neutral oil

2 to 3 tablespoons green curry paste (see Note)

1½ cups full-fat coconut milk

½ cup vegetable stock

3 tablespoons fish sauce, plus more as needed

2 tablespoons grated palm sugar, plus more as needed

½ Thai bird's eye chile, sliced (optional; use only if you crave HEAT)

8 Thai eggplants, quartered

8 cremini mushrooms, halved

6 makrut lime leaves, lightly bruised and torn in half

1 cup Thai basil

Cooked jasmine rice (don't sub plain rice here) for serving

½ cup cilantro leaves

1 red serrano chile, thinly sliced

Lime wedges for garnish

Thai cuisine is another major food obsession of mine. So, on my first trip to Thailand, I enrolled in a cooking class, where I learned dishes such as tom yam, papaya salad, and this green curry. The curry in particular was so revolutionary. It's so deep and dank, and I assumed that it would take hours of slow simmering to create these layers of flavor. I was blown away to learn that it comes together really quickly—you can make an unreal dish in less than an hour. The key is finding all the right ingredients, especially Thai eggplants and makrut lime leaves. They're essential in this recipe, so find a Thai grocer—they'll also have the curry paste, coconut milk, Thai basil, and palm sugar. As always, be super-careful when handling bird's eye chiles—these guys are so spicy. You can seed it if you like it a little less spicy, or keep the seeds (and even use a whole chile!) if you like it more spicy. Either way, wear plastic gloves or at least wash your hands *realllly* well. I feel like the heat is part of the experience. You want to get that blast of chile that almost makes you break out in a sweat, but quickly mellows, making you salivate for the next bite.

Use this recipe as your jumping-off point. If you want to get wild with it, you can add a protein, like thinly sliced boneless skinless chicken thighs, or additional veggies, like carrots or even potatoes, which aren't necessarily traditional but are definitely yum. Pair with a cold dry Riesling or a Singha beer to cool you down.

1 In a wok, deep saucepan, or Dutch oven over medium heat, warm the oil, then add the curry paste and fry until your kitchen starts smelling VERY GOOD, about 2 minutes. Add the coconut milk, veggie stock, fish sauce, and sugar and stir until the curry paste dissolves. Bring to a boil, then turn down the heat until the sauce simmers.

2 Add the bird's eye chile (if using) and eggplants to the curry and simmer until they soften a bit, 5 to 7 minutes. Add the mushrooms, cook 2 minutes more, and then add the lime leaves and basil and cook for 3 minutes. Now taste for seasoning; is it boring? Does it need a funky kick? Add a li'l more fish sauce. Is it too spicy and sharp? If so, add a li'l sugar.

3 Serve the curry over jasmine rice (it's all about this combo of gently fragrant jasmine rice and the deep, dank curry) and garnish with cilantro leaves, a few slices of serrano chile, and lime wedges.

Note: There's a lot of variation between brands of curry paste. If you're using an imported Thai brand, you'll probably need only 2 tablespoons. Some mass American brands are a little less potent, so you might want to bump it up to 3 tablespoons. My recommendation is always to start with less and stir in more to taste, if you feel like your curry needs it.

TINGLE TAGINE

MAKES 4 TO 6 SERVINGS

Here's a recipe for all my Veggie Chippies! Love you. Chef's Bow.

This dish is inspired by my buds' birthday dinners at Marrakesh restaurant in Philadelphia. I love the ritual of eating there. First you start with warm rose water to clean your hands, since there are no utensils. Then they send out dish after dish of incredible Moroccan delicacies: b'stella, lemon chicken, lamb tagine. By the time the belly dancers arrive, I am in an extremely elevated state of bliss. They also let us smoke weed in there, so it is extra trippy.

I love this dish because of its one-pot communal aspect. The spices and ginger and preserved lemon give the fresh tingle that I crave so much in these preparations. The tagine is both the cooking vessel and the serving dish, and it's so beautiful to look at. It's also especially great for preparing meat dishes that require hours of slow cooking. The steam rises and condenses at the top of the vessel, then rehydrates your food, creating a super-flavorful and moist stew. You can use a tagine for this recipe, or you can use a Dutch oven. But I highly recommend buying a tagine and getting INTO the EXPERIENCE.

1 In a tagine, deep saucepan, or Dutch oven over medium-low heat, warm the olive oil. Add the onion and a pinch of salt and sauté until translucent, about 5 minutes. Add the garlic, ginger, cinnamon, coriander, sumac, turmeric, cayenne, black pepper, saffron and its soaking liquid, and 1 tablespoon salt and stir until fragrant, 1 to 2 minutes. Stir in the carrots, potatoes, tomatoes, veg stock, chickpeas, preserved lemon, and apricots and bring to a simmer.

2 Cover the cooking vessel with its lid and cook over low heat for 30 minutes. Add the cauliflower, stir to combine, and cover the cooking vessel again. Cook until the vegetables are tender and can be pierced easily with a fork, 20 to 30 minutes more. Taste and adjust the seasoning, adding more salt as needed.

3 While the tagine is cooking, in a small saucepan over medium heat, toast the almond slices just until golden, 1 to 2 minutes.

4 Plate the tagine over rice and garnish with the toasted almonds, mint, and lime pickle (if using) before serving.

¼ cup extra-virgin olive oil

1 yellow onion, sliced ⅛ inch thick

Kosher salt

4 garlic cloves, sliced

2 tablespoons minced ginger

1 cinnamon stick

1 teaspoon ground coriander

1 teaspoon sumac

1 teaspoon ground turmeric

½ teaspoon cayenne pepper

¼ teaspoon freshly ground black pepper

1 pinch saffron, soaked in 2 tablespoons warm water for 15 minutes

5 carrots, peeled and cut into 1-inch pieces

4 creamer potatoes, quartered

One 14-ounce can whole tomatoes, crushed by hand

1 cup vegetable stock

1 cup canned chickpeas, drained

½ preserved lemon, pulp removed and skin thinly sliced into strips

½ cup dried apricots halves, chopped

½ head cauliflower, separated into florets

½ cup sliced almonds

Cooked white rice for serving

Chopped mint for garnish

Lime pickle (this is an Indian condiment and will add that extra TINGLE!) for garnish (optional)

LIFE-SAVING SMOOTHIE

MAKES 1 SERVING

¾ cup coconut water

½ apple, chopped

1-inch knob fresh ginger, peeled and sliced into coins (more if you feel a cold coming on)

2 big kale leaves, ribbed and torn

1 cup spinach

1 handful fresh seasonal fruit (such as strawberries, raspberries, or blueberries; optional)

1 tablespoon powdered vitamin C (this helps all the good stuff really absorb into your system)

2 ice cubes

There's a reason this is the last recipe in the chapter. It's because this is my secret weapon, the key you'll need to fully unlock the Heimy Lifestyle.

After eating tons of fried chicken and rich braises and cheesy pizza, you're gonna need something green and healthful to keep your body happy. That's why I drink one of these smoothies a few times a week. When I first moved to California, I had awful chronic allergies—this smoothie even helped with that. It is truly lifesaving.

If you have been pounding the booze, add a beet to this recipe; it will help your liver.

1 In a blender, combine the coconut water, apple, ginger, kale, spinach, fruit (if using), vitamin C, and ice cubes and puree, adding a bit of water as needed to reach your desired consistency.

2 Pour into a glass, drink, and let the healing begin.

PRIVATE PARTY

When I first started dating Madi, she was always VERY impressed by my ability to pull together a delicious snack plate at a moment's notice. Always have delicious snackers on hand. The best and easiest is tinned fish, which are known as *conservas* in Spain. In the event of a nuclear apocalypse, my fallout shelter will be filled with tins of plump mussels and clams, tiny sardines, and flavorful octopus, all packed in oil and sealed so they'll last forever. In the meantime, I like to dip into my stash whenever I'm craving a salty sea treat.

Keep in mind this has nothing to do with sad, water-packed cans of tuna from your childhood. In Spain and Portugal, there is a nearly two-century tradition of fishermen taking their freshest and best catch and then, just a few hours after harvest, sealing it in a tin for indefinite storage. It's a perfect way to preserve seafood at the peak of its freshness, plus, you don't need to keep it cold. Look for conservas in specialty shops or order online from Regalis Foods.

MY FAVORITE FISHIES

Berberechos (cockles)

Bonito (tuna)

Boquerones (white anchovies)

Mejillones (mussels in escabeche)

Pulpo (octopus)

Sardinillas (baby sardines)

Tinta (squid in its ink; sometimes called chipirón, which refers to baby squid)

THE ULTIMATE SNACK PLATE

Mini baguettes smeared with soft French butter and topped with anchovies

A combo of fresh and dried fruit—grapes, sliced apples, kumquats, dried apricots

Hard and soft cheeses

One really nice type of charcuterie

Bonk conservas!

SMALL HORSE
CHAPTER

WINE-HEIM

2019 Pinot Noir Rosé
Kabinett trocken

Many people are intimidated by wine culture,

because they feel as though they don't know where to start. So, in the interest of full disclosure, I am going to tell you exactly where I started: drinking nasty, warm beer out of a plastic BeerBall in the woods.

If you were a teenager in the '90s, you probably remember the BeerBall, or Party Ball, as Bud Light liked to call it. Basically, it was a 5-gallon plastic sphere with a tap. I remember the first time my friends and I encountered one at a party. We couldn't believe it! We were in love. It was gorgeous and circular and, most important, it seemed to have an endless supply of beer.

We'd drink it over the course of a weekend, out in the woods where we'd hide it under some leaves. Of course there was no refrigeration, and by the end it was so skunky and disgusting.

Once it was drained, the fun was just beginning. That deflated plastic sphere became our new best friend. We would hug it, kick it around for sport, and eventually toss it into some other kid's yard for their parents to find on Monday morning.

When we were lucky, one of us would sneak a jug of Almaden—it was basically the Carlo Rossi of the time—from their parents' garage. That was my first introduction to wine, and that upscale jug shape made me feel so sophisticated. Until we started beer-bonging the wine. That was a low point of my drinking evolution, tied with the time I had a two-day hangover after pounding Zima Black all night at a techno dance party in Shibuya, Tokyo.

Then I moved to North Philly for film school, where we switched from beer to forties—Colt 45, Olde English, Cobra, and Laser were my favorites. Malt beverages gave you an extra kick that made a warm summer night in Philly that much more beautiful. On special occasions we'd invest in a box of Franzia wine. We curated a lot of art and film "experiences" and needed some sort of semi-wine to class up the place. Franzia was the best we could do on our limited budget, but I knew it was gross, even then. My comedy partner and roommate, Tim Heidecker, and I would buy cases of Cream Ale 16-ouncers and return the bottles for a refill the next day. It was all about the most bang for your buck back then.

Once I started working as an assistant to wedding photographers and had a few dollars in my wallet, I got more serious about food and wine. This also coincided with my obsession with *The Sopranos*. Before new episodes would air on Sundays, we'd cook a big pasta dinner and drink bottles of Ruffino Chianti, Tony Soprano's favorite. From there, I got really into Sangiovese, the main grape in Chianti, and then graduated to Super Tuscans, which are pricey, big flavor-bomb wines made from nonnative grapes, like Merlot and Cabernet Franc. Just like Tony, I thought bigger was better. I NEEDED that full-bodied bravado to stand up to my baked ziti!

I am not telling you all of this because I secretly want to bring back the BeerBall. I am telling you this to show that no one is born with incredible taste in booze. Learning to appreciate wine and craft beer and fine spirits is an evolution. I *make* wine with my partner, Joel Burt, and yet I'm still learning about it every day. Even the greatest wine experts in the world will admit that it's an ever-evolving genre, and that they're constantly learning new things.

In this chapter, my goal is to teach you some wine fundamentals so that you can go into a restaurant or wine bar or shop and ask questions with confidence. I'll share a few of the things that excite me the most, like how to open a bottle of bubbles with a sword (see page 248) and the best wine to pair with burgers (see page 244).

I used to think that wine was pretentious, something only for the elite. Then, through my travels, I realized it's a part of daily life in so many cultures; like in Italy, where wine is more important than water. It's an everyday, small indulgence that brings family and friends together. So, now, I live by the principles I learned in Italy and France: Wine is as important to me as the meal. Sometimes it's a simple village wine, and other times it's crazy Grand Cru Burgundy. I embrace them all, as long as that wine is made with love.

If you're still feeling nervous about embarking on your own wine journey, just remember that I was once a teenager drinking skunky beer out of a ball. We all gotta start somewhere. My hope is that reading this will pique your curiosity and inspire you to start drinking some delicious wine.

What I Look for in a Wine

I remember the bottle that changed everything for me.

It was Dard et Ribo's Saint-Joseph, a Syrah from the northern Rhône region of France. I was in Paris and had just finished one of the most revolutionary meals of my life at Iñaki Aizpitarte's Le Chateaubriand. My friends and I got a tip to visit Le Verre Volé after dinner to buy a bottle to drink by the Canal St-Martin.

At Le Verre Volé, we gushed about our life-changing meal and tried to remember all the wines we drank. We were dizzy with excitement. The bartender recommended, as a nightcap, a bottle of Syrah from producers Dard et Ribo. Politely and respectfully, we accepted, but I was apprehensive: I'd never had a Syrah that I enjoyed before.

But this bottle was so different from the heavy, one-note Syrahs that I was used to. It was juicy, light, and full of energy. It had life! It was magic. It was also relatively low alcohol—13 percent alcohol by volume, or ABV, rather than 15 or 16 percent like so many American wines. This may seem like a small difference but it greatly affects the weight of the wine. It didn't bring me down as I drank it; it made me elated. I slammed it out of the bottle and I was HOOKED.

Afterward, I started researching what made that bottle so special—why it, and other wines like it, allowed me to drink wine all evening without that "I'm done with red wine" feeling. What I learned is that Dard et Ribo specializes in organic, low-intervention viniculture—known as natural wine.

Natural wine is a loaded term, and a lot of people debate its true meaning. So, I try to be more specific when I talk about the style of wine that I personally gravitate toward: low-intervention wines made from grapes that are grown organically and harvested conscientiously by smaller, independent winemakers who have a unique vision.

"Low-intervention" is basically a nice way of saying that the wines haven't been fucked with in the cellar. Have you ever noticed that there isn't an ingredients list on the back of wine bottles? It's pretty messed up, because there are more than seventy additives legally allowed by the USDA in wine. You might go to a fancy grocery store and buy beautiful organic produce and sustainable meat and assume that the wine

they sell is organic and sustainable, too, but you'd be wrong. A lot of the wine on grocery store shelves—even fancy grocery stores—is "conventional" wine, made on an industrial scale from grapes that are farmed using pesticides and bought on the commodity market, with chemicals and colorants added in the cellar.

The main point of all this is that the natural wines I discovered at the beginning of my wine journey made me feel good. I could taste LIFE in the bottle. I had fewer hangovers. My body and palate weren't exhausted by glass number two. I felt connected to the people making the wine. And the wines themselves transported me to the place where they were produced. I loved discovering that

ME AND JOEL BURT, MY
PARTNER AT LAS JARAS

each vintage was different and that I could taste these slight variations in the wine from year to year. It was a far cry from the flat, lifeless, commercial wines that taste exactly the same no matter the vintage.

I dove headfirst into the world of natural wine. I visited natural wine fairs and wine bars around the globe. I met producers, importers, and sommeliers who helped guide my journey. I tasted some wines that I loved and moved me on a spiritual level. I tasted some wines that I really *didn't* love. And that's what it's all about. You find your zone, you evolve, and you keeping tasting and learning.

Today, I'm really drawn to wines that speak to the place in which they were made. I want a wine that tells me something about the person who made it, the land where the grapes were grown, and the region's winemaking history and traditions. I'm looking for *terroir*. You've probably heard this word before. It doesn't have a direct translation in English, but it describes the many factors—soil, climate, history, geography, culture—that make a wine what it is.

Here's an example. When I pop a bottle of Etna Rosso, a wine made in the shadows of Mount Etna in Sicily, I can taste that rugged countryside in my glass. I smell the volcanic ash that makes the soil there so fertile. I feel the heat of the sun. I taste the age of the vines. That's the power of terroir to me.

There is a connection between low-intervention wines and wines that express terroir. That's what I'm into. What I'm *not* into are certain winemaking styles that obscure the pure expression of the grape. Some California winemakers wait to harvest until really late in the growing season, when the grapes have been baking in the sun all summer and have become super-ripe and sugary—almost raisin-y. The resulting wine is sweet and intensely alcoholic. Then they age the wine in brand-new oak barrels (or worse, they add oak chips to the wine) so that the wines have this over-the-top oaky flavor. Those types of interventions just break Heimy's heart. There's no finesse! What you end up with is a boozy fruit bomb that totally obscures its terroir.

At Las Jaras, we take a different approach. Joel is the winemaker and, while he and I don't own vineyards, we partner with farmers whom we know and respect, who grow grape varieties that are well suited to their climate and land. Joel lives in Sonoma County and works closely with the farmers to decide just the right moment to harvest, typically much earlier in the season than other big California brands. As we have grown as a company, we have convinced some of the growers to convert to certified organic farming if we purchase all of our fruit from them. It's good for us and good for the earth! When it comes to vinifying the grapes, we rely on native yeasts for fermentation. We don't add any colorants or flavor enhancers, and the only preservative we ever use is sulfur dioxide (a natural preservative that has been used in winemaking since ancient Roman times), which we add to some of our bottles in very small amounts. I think that is what makes our wine beautiful and special. It's a *natural* product in that it's tied to the earth. We make wine this way because it's the style of wine we love to drink. It's fresh, lively, balanced, and, most important, freaking delicious.

If you've read this far, you're probably getting thirsty and wondering when I'm gonna teach you how to find beautiful, well-made wine out in the wild. Don't worry, Heimy's got you! Keep reading. In the next few pages, I'll share a few of my secrets on finding great wines to drink at home, at restaurants, and out in the wider world.

Wine 101: A Beginner's Guide to Becoming a Wine Freak

The only guaranteed way to learn about wine is to drink A LOT of wine. So that's my biggest piece of advice to you—drink more wine! Taste lots of different wines; ask questions; try to remember what you drank and what you liked (or didn't like) about it. The more wine you drink, the better you'll understand the characteristics of wines made from different grapes and in different regions. "Okay, I really like all the red wines I'm drinking from the Beaujolais region of France." "I thought I liked Pinot Noir, but this Pinot Noir from France tastes really different from that Pinot Noir from Oregon." "I thought I didn't like Riesling, but both of the German bottles labeled 'Kabinett' that I tried were really good."

I'm a big note guy and my phone is filled with photos of bottles I've enjoyed and notes about them. So I encourage you to get into that kind of organization. It's nerdy but necessary. You'll be rewarded later, especially if someone asks you what wines you like from a certain region—you can just pull up some examples from your notes. There are also some great wine apps that tell you all sorts of info (producer, region, grape varieties, vintage, etc.) about a wine just by scanning the label.

Something I realized on my wine journey is that taste changes over time. I feel like mine changes every six months. So it's really important to keep an open mind and to be prepared to revisit wines on this adventure. I thought I hated Riesling because the only bottles I'd tasted were lifeless and cloyingly sweet. But then my friend J.D.

Plotnick turned me on to producers Veyder-Malberg and Keller, and that shattered my assumptions. These gorgeous Rieslings are all about electrifying acid that balances any residual sugar to create a masterpiece in the glass. Wow! Now I LOVE Riesling!

To become a full-fledged wine freak, you have to immerse yourself into the wine world. Follow restaurants, wine bars, sommeliers, winemakers, and Top Food Blogs, like mine, on social media. Buy some books on classic and natural wine. Go to tastings at your local wine shop. Start to notice the importers listed on the back of wine bottles you like. Start a wine club with your buddies. Get everyone to bring a bottle from the same region and cook something to go along with the wine, like ragù with Nebbiolo or oysters with Chablis. Talk about what you're tasting. Have fun and go deep.

ERIC'S ESSENTIALS (WINE EDITION)

1. **You only need one wine opener!** Throw out that bunny-ear wine opener, aerator, and any of the weird wine gadgets you got from your Secret Santa, because all you need is one wine opener: The super-classic "server's friend" style wine key. It's classic for a reason—it works!

2. **Invest in a portable wine cooler.** Show up to the beach or barbecue ready to drink! There's nothing worse than making your friends find you a space in their crowded fridge, or waiting 'til the last minute to try to chill down your wine.

3. **Get a li'l wine fridge if you are going to do any aging.** Store bottles on their sides to keep the cork wet. If you aren't going to splurge on a separate wine fridge, store all of your wine— even reds—in your normal fridge. At the very least, keep your wine out of the sunlight and in a cool area, especially if you are drinking natural wine. Heat and light are your enemy!

4. **Serve your wine at the proper temp.** Experts will tell you the ideal serving temp for white wine is 50° to 55°F—warmer than fridge temp— and for red wine is between 62° and 68°F—cooler than room temp. I drink my casual white wines very cold. Finer wines, I serve a bit warmer and let them continue to warm up in the glass. The colder the wine, the harder it is to smell and taste, which is why you will start to notice the wine opening up and expressing itself as it warms. I always serve reds with a slight chill to start, then allow to warm in the glass.

Wine Regions
I LOVE

There is so much good wine being made in so many countries right now, it's hard to pick just a few. The following list is specific to me and my personal tastes at the moment—these are the wines and places that most excite me.

FRANCE

I gotta start this section by talking about *Burgundy*, basically the Holy Land for fine wine. (Cistercian monks started making wine here a millennium ago.) In Burgundy, red wine is made from Pinot Noir; white wine, primarily from Chardonnay. The highest-end Burgundies (which are classified as Grand Cru) are made in tiny amounts; and each year, wine drinkers around the globe fight over buying them. This is part of the reason why they are so rare and expensive! But on special, *special* occasions, it's worth the splurge and will kind of ruin you for all other wine!

Chanterêves: There are so many incredible, historic domaines in Burgundy, some of which have been in the same family for centuries. For this reason, people sometimes forget to keep an eye out for new producers. Chanterêves, made by husband-and-wife team Guillaume and Tomoko, was launched relatively recently (in 2010), yet they are making some of my favorite wines in Burgundy right now!

Domaine de Villaine: Aubert de Villaine, co-owner and co-director of Domaine de la Romanée-Conti (DRC), is basically the most famous Burgundian winemaker in the world. DRC is the most culty and expensive wine there is, but de Villaine feels a moral imperative to make a more affordable and accessible wine as well, which is why I love to recommend his Bouzeron Aligoté. Aligoté is considered the "lesser" of Burgundy's white wine grapes (it's always overshadowed by Chardonnay), but in the hands of a master such as de Villaine, it's so beautiful.

Domaine Hubert Lamy: Probably my favorite producer of white wine in Burgundy. Olivier Lamy works in Saint-Aubin, an appellation that doesn't have the historical reputation of Meursault and Puligny-Montrachet, which means the wines are a bit more accessible. His winemaking is so damn spot-on; and when you get a good bottle, it's a magical experience. Huge, long, transcendent finishes that make me almost pass out with joy.

Maison des Joncs: If you find these wines, you MUST snatch them. Jae Chu was born in Seoul, Korea, but her deep passion for wine took her to France, where she interned with iconic producers and eventually made her own wine—in tiny quantities, and only two vintages (2017 and 2018) before becoming head winemaker at a historic château in the Rhône. Chu's Burgundy is such a special and thoughtfully made wine, I feel privileged to have tasted it.

Maison MC Thiriet: I met Camille Thiriet in San Francisco at a wine event called La Paulée. In a room filled with hot shots and grand masters of Burgundy, we were both on the younger side, and bonded over our passion for Burgundian wines. Later, I was lucky enough to visit the winery, which was in the garage of the grand Château de Comblanchien, a few kilometers south of Nuits-Saint-Georges. Keep an eye out for these fresh, elegant wines.

Domaine Simon Bize & Fils: This historic domaine was founded in 1880 in Savigny-lès-Beaune, considered by many to be an underrated region of Burgundy. Today, the domaine is run by Chisa Bize and Marielle Bize-Grivot. Considering how much of a boys' club Burgundy is, I love to support and drink wines made by vigneronnes (female winemakers).

Domaine Sylvain Pataille: Historically, Marsannay was one of the less prized and appreciated appellations of Burgundy. For that reason, its wines are somewhat more accessible and affordable than others in the Côte de Nuits. Sylvain Pataille got his start as a famous consultant to many domaines in Burgundy and then started making his own brilliant wines in Marsannay—red, white, and even a rosé (Marsannay is the only appellation in Burgundy that allows all three).

If I had to pick one desert-island wine, it would be a crisp white Chablis with a long lingering saline finish. *Chablis* is the northernmost pocket of Burgundy, and its Chardonnay wines are utterly unique in the world of wine: steely, bracing, and electrifying, with a mineral complexity and elegant austerity that moves me every time. Perhaps it's the marginal climate (being so far north, Chablis can have long, hard winters); perhaps it's the fact that it lies on a former seabed, so the soil is filled with teeny, fossilized oyster shells. But there's something magic in the land. It brings me to tears of joy just thinking about drinking that wine while floating on a raft in clear blue water by a white sand beach with no one around. Just me and my cold bottle of chabbles.

Domaine Alice et Olivier De Moor: Natural winemaking is not so common in Chablis, but the De Moors make beautiful, expressive, low-intervention wines that are classic in style but have integrity. They also do magic with Aligoté. I love these wines.

Domaine Moreau-Naudet: Another low-intervention producer making electric Chardonnay. I first tasted Moreau-Naudet at Lou Wine in Los Angeles—it was one of those game-changing bottles.

Domaine Raveneau: This isn't just peak Chablis; it's peak wine for me. But these days it's also one of the most sought-after wines in the world, and I just can't afford it. Maybe you'll send me some for Chrimbus if I'm a good boy?

Domaine Jean Collet et Fils: Classic expressions from a family with roots in Chablis dating back to the late 1700s.

Thierry Richoux: Richoux works in Irancy, a village a few kilometers from Chablis, where he makes gorgeous red wines.

Another favorite French wine region is the *Loire Valley*, which is large and has such a diversity of wines. A lot of experimental and arty winemakers have gravitated to this area, which is why there are so many cool natural wines coming from there right now. But it is also home to some of the most beautiful and elegant classic expressions; for example, the Chenin Blanc–based white wines of Savennières,

the high-acid saline white wines of Muscadet, or the earthy Cabernet Franc–based red wines of Chinon.

Domaine Arnaud Lambert: Mineral-driven Chenin Blanc and Cabernet Franc, and a brilliant expression of the Brézé Hill, one of the most historic and important wine terroirs in France. The "Clos David" bottling is one of my favorite Chenin Blancs—hell, I'll say it, one of my favorite white wines!

Domaine Guiberteau: Also in Brézé, also making gorg Chenin Blanc. I talk a lot about "electricity" in white wines. If you want to know what I'm talking about, try Romain Guiberteau's wines.

Richard Leroy: The master of Chenin Blanc. These wines are culty and hard to find; but if you do, you're in for such a treat.

One of the first wine regions I ever visited was the *Jura* on the easternmost edge of France, nestled between Burgundy and Switzerland. Historically this has been pretty remote, rustic farming country, and the wines weren't very popular. They mostly got consumed by the people who lived there. But now the secret is out, and Jura has so many beautiful, high-quality wines (the best-of-the

best Chardonnays give Burgundy a run for its money, for a fraction of the price). In addition to familiar grapes, like Chard and Pinot Noir, I love the Jura's native red grapes, Trousseau and Poulsard, which make light-bodied red wines that are a perfect pairing for Thanksgiving dinner.

André et Mireille Tissot: Biodynamic winemaking in a range of styles—don't miss the sparkling crémant, white wines made from Chardonnay and Savagnin, and reds with traditional Jura grapes, like Poulsard and Trousseau.

Domaine Labet: Beautiful, meditative Chardonnay that I think stands up to white Burgundy any day.

Domaine de l'Octavin: Fun natural wines made by the wildly talented Alice Bouvot. I consider her more artist than winemaker, and that's a huge compliment. I slammed many a bottle of her Troll wines when I first started my wine journey. She's also just the loveliest person.

Beautiful *Beaujolais*! This region is considered the birthplace of the contemporary natural wine movement, which is part of the reason why I drank a lot of this stuff early in my natural wine voyage. I was excited by the light-bodied

style, which pairs so wonderfully with so many foods and has a poppy punch from its unique style of fermentation, called carbonic maceration. The red wines from this region are made from Gamay, which I love to chill and then allow to warm slightly on the table. (Yes, *chilled* red wine. Trust!)

Anne-Sophie Dubois: Dubois worked in and was inspired by Burgundy but applied what she learned to Gamay. She's part of a new generation of winemakers in Beaujolais who are pushing things in interesting ways.

Domaine Thillardon: Paul-Henri Thillardon is working in Chénas, a more under-the-radar corner of Beaujolais. He was mentored by Dutraive and Métras (see following entries), and his wines are zippy, clean, and lovely.

Domaine de la Grand'Cour: Jean-Louis Dutraive works in Fleurie, a cru whose name translates to "flowery," which is especially wild because the wines *do* have this beautiful and distinctive floral aroma. Just a beautiful red wine.

Yvon Métras: Another master of Fleurie, a total legend making legendary wines. Find an older vintage. If it's a good bottle, it really holds up and becomes this incredible explosion of flavors.

Last but never least, we've gotta talk about *Champagne*! Because I love bubbs. Right now I'm into "grower Champagnes," which are made by smaller operations that grow their own grapes (rather than buying them in bulk from farmers, which is what a lot of the big-name Champagne houses do). Because

of all the marketing hype, a lot of people don't think of Champagne as a "real" wine. This is so wrong. Artisanal, grower Champagne is such a beautiful thing and one of the most versatile food wines in existence.

Agrapart: This is my go-to celebration Champagne, but it also works well with so many different types of food. Fried chicken and Agrapart is pure magic.

Francis Boulard: Don't forget about rosé Champers! The one made by Boulard is one of my faves.

Georges Laval: One of my favorite examples of the principles of natural winemaking being applied to Champagne. Vincent Laval makes jaw-droppingly beautiful Champagne from his tiny, five-acre plot in Cumières. Laval is noted for his non-interventionist approach—indigenous yeasts, low sulfur, no dosage; he even plows much of the land by horse.

Jacques Lassaigne: Emmanuel Lassaigne helped popularize the idea of vinifiying grapes from single parcels (as opposed to the then more common practice in Champagne of blending wines from many different parcels), which makes his wines extra-special and a beautiful articulation of the individual terroirs of the region.

Le Closerie: Made by modern-day legend Jérôme Prévost, from grapes grown on soils that have the same teeny marine fossils as Chablis, resulting in a crisp, mineral-y dream wine.

ITALY

Planted on the misty hills of *Piedmont* in northern Italy—in regions such as Barolo, Carema, Barbaresco, and Ghemme—the Nebbiolo grape produces one of the greatest red wines in the world. It's bold and assertive and its wines are very tannic and acidic. But if you buy a beautiful Barolo or Barbaresco and have the patience to age it for many years (decades, even), you will be rewarded with one of the most bonk wines imaginable. It pairs perfectly with so many of my favorite Italian dishes, like wild boar ragù and pasta with shaved truffles. What else can I say? These wines are killer.

Canonica: Giovanni Canonica runs a small agriturismo (an amazing Italian institution of farm/hostels, where you basically get to stay in a beautiful, rustic working farm; highly recommend) in Barolo, where he makes just a small amount of truly outstanding wine in the cellars below.

Fabio Gea: Genre-pushing natural red and rosato wines from small parcels in Barbaresco, made mostly with Nebbiolo but also Dolcetto and Barbera.

Luigi Spertino: Mauro Spertino works in Asti, in the northeastern part of Piedmont, where he makes a beautiful Barbera. If you can find it, his vermouth is super-special too.

Poderi Colla: A brilliant family-run operation with deep roots in the region, making classic, elegant Barolo and Barbaresco in the same way their relatives did in the 1960s.

Rovellotti: Just a perfect example of the wines of Ghemme, made by a family with roots in the region dating back to the fifteenth(!) century.

I've come a long way since my time drinking Ruffino Chianti while watching *The Sopranos.* Nowadays I'm into only natural wines from *Chianti*, made primarily from the Sangiovese grape.

I Fabbri: Great, low-intervention Chiantis made in small quantities by the Grassi sisters.

Val delle Corti: Fun, drinkable Chianti made by Roberto and Lis Bianchi in the Radda area. Also check out their rosato.

One of my favorite places on Earth is the Amalfi Coast, south of Naples on the west coast of Italy. That's why I have such a soft spot for the white wines of the *Campania* region.

Cantina Giardino: I love this project from a group of six friends who decided they wanted to make a range of natural wines that preserve old vineyards and celebrate native regional varieties such as Aglianico, Coda di Volpe, Greco, and Fiano. Local artists design the beautiful labels, which get a Chef's Kiss from me—you know I love wine/art collabs.

Cantine dell'Angelo: Angelo Muto is a master of Greco di Tufo, a wine that immediately transports me to the seaside restaurants of the Amalfi Coast. So many happy memories, so much tasty wine.

Don Chisciotte: Beautiful, natural white wine made from the Fiano grape.

Podere Veneri Vecchio: Raffaello Annichiarico was making natural wine before it was cool, using indigenous yeasts and home-made fertilizers and other natural preparations.

GERMANY AND AUSTRIA

If I can convince you of one thing, it's that you have to give Riesling a chance. It's such a misunderstood grape. In the hands of true masters, Riesling is one of the most complex and expressive wines in the world, with electric acidity and the potential to age for years and years. Two of my favorite regions are *Mosel* in Germany and the *Wachau* in Austria. Many of the vineyards are planted on insanely steep and precarious slopes, literally carved into stone, overlooking the Mosel and Danube rivers, respectively. I think a big part of the confusion with Riesling is that there are several styles, ranging from dry (a technical term that means there is no residual sugar left over from fermentation) to sweet, and from very light in body (Kabinett and Spätlese) to heavier (with Eiswein, or ice wine, being the most dramatic example). A lot of people are afraid of sweetness in wines. But please, listen to Heimy and buy a bottle of high-quality German Riesling, which might have some residual sugar, and tell me it isn't the most balanced and beautiful wine ever. Balance is all about that dramatic tension between the searing acidity and subtle sweetness.

Keller: Wine-writing legend Jancis Robinson once called the Keller wines "German Montrachets"— comparing them to the greatest white wine of Burgundy. I think it's a fair comparison!

Peter Lauer: One of my favorites from the Saar region of Germany. Lauer makes wines that are super-intense and flavorful but somehow still light and lift you up rather than weigh you down.

Veyder-Malberg: Beautiful, elegant, hard-to-get-your-hands-on Austrian Riesling from the iconic Wachau region.

GREECE

On the Greek island of *Santorini*, they make one of the most refreshing white wines in the world, Assyrtiko, from ancient vineyards. It's such an intensely dry, mineral wine. I love it with seafood; it tastes like lemons and sunshine. My friend, artist Chloe Wise, took me on an epic four-wheeler ride down the shoreline of Santorini. We looked up on the bluffs and saw rows and rows of Assyrtiko vines. It was so breathtaking, and I think about that moment anytime I pop a bottle Stateside.

Hatzidakis Winery: Natural-leaning producer making gorgeous golden Assyrtiko.

UNITED STATES OF AMERICA

California was cool in the 1960s and '70s, and now it is again, fifty years later! But when I first started drinking wine in the '90s, most of the stuff coming from California was big, over-the-top flavor bombs with no subtlety and no finesse. In the last ten to fifteen years things have changed, and the magic of the '60s and '70s is coming back. Now there is a new generation of producers who are making wine in a more restrained, elegant style. Through my work with Las Jaras, I've been lucky enough to meet and befriend a lot of these winemakers. They are kind of the indie musicians of the wine scene (whereas those big, corporate wine labels from the '90s were more like commercial pop—catering to the masses).

Ceritas Wines: The most elegant, electrifying Chardonnay and Pinot Noir you can find in California today, from some of the best and most historic vineyards in Sonoma County.

Lo-Fi Wines: Bright, drinkable natural wines from the Santa Barbara and Paso Robles areas. What's up, Mike!

Martha Stoumen Wines: Natural wine but in the classic style, often leaning toward Italian varieties, like Nero d'Avola. Las Jaras got to collaborate with Martha on a 100 percent Valdiguié pét-nat that's always been a fave of mine.

Methode Sauvage and Iruai: Two labels by natural winemaker Chad Hinds. Methode Sauvage specializes in Chenin Blanc and Cabernet Franc, two of my favorite Loire Valley varieties. Iruai is a bit more experimental, with Chad making Alpine-style wines from Alpine native varieties planted in the northern reaches of California, near Oregon.

Ridge Vineyards: Paul Draper and his project, Ridge, is just the best classic California wine around. Draper stayed the course and made restrained, nuanced wines all through the 1980s and '90s. That's why it's always worth investing in a bottle of Ridge with some age on it, if you can find it.

Ruth Lewandowski: I really dig Lewandowski's "Feints," a lush coferment of red and white Piedmontese varieties that results in a super-drinkable light red/dark rosé.

Most of the grapes we use at Las Jaras come from Sonoma County, California. But a few years ago, we made wine with beautiful Pinot Noir harvested from the Chehalem Mountains of *Oregon*. I was completely blown away by the depth and elegance of this wine. As vineyard land becomes more and more expensive in California, and as the climate gets hotter and hotter, with wildfires that make winegrowing difficult and dangerous, a lot of people are looking north to Oregon. It's a region that has so much potential, and already there are so many creative winemakers making beautiful wines.

Swick Wines: Natural wines made from all sorts of fun varieties, from Pinot Noir to Touriga Nacional. Every vintage, I'm blown away by Joe Swick's prolific range of goodies.

Maloof Wines: I have to give a shout-out to the collaboration between Bee Maloof and my pal Joe Beddia. They made a Beddia Bianco from carbonic Chardonnay that is Chef's Kiss Deep Bow delicioso!

Minimus: Cool, experimental wines by Chad Stock. Usually I like to keep things traditional, but Chad's exploration of different aging vessels (cigar barrels, amphora) and rare grape varieties just works.

St. Reginald Parish: Low-intervention wines in the classic style from cooler-climate sites in the Willamette Valley. Much love and respect to their winemaker, my buddy Andy. Tiny Tuesdays, here we come!

AUSTRALIA

If all you know is Shiraz and Yellow Tail, prepare to have your mind blown. The Aussies have one of the wildest and most vibrant natural wine scenes in the world right now, and these wines are just starting to make it to the US market.

Gentle Folk Wines: Natural wine from the beautiful Adelaide Hills. If you can find it, try their cider too.

Ochota Barrels: The winemaker, Taras, recently and tragically passed away. He was a legend and pushed Australian wine in important directions, seeking out old-vine sites and making electric Grenache and Syrah that will make you rethink what those grapes are really about. He was the closest thing to our spiritual brother at Las Jaras in terms of style and philosophy.

Patrick Sullivan: Beautiful natural wines from grapes planted on volcanic soils.

How to Shop for Wine

It's so much easier to find good wine than it used to be. Shopping for wine today is heavenly compared to the nightmare I grew up with in Philly. (It's a long story, but basically all alcohol sales in Pennsylvania are controlled by the state, which means you have to go to state-run stores, which always have annoying hours and a bad selection.) Nowadays there's a new natural wine bar or shop popping up on every block.

The key to shopping for wine is to find a spot you trust, where you can build the all-important wine buyer/customer relationship. A good wine shop has friendly staff who love to chitchat. They'll ask you about what you like and point you toward new things. My favorite shops offer tastings that focus on a specific region or producer. It's an affordable way to try a bunch of bottles before buying.

When you're in the wine shop, don't be afraid to ask questions. "I'm making roast chicken for dinner; what should I pair it with?" "I like juicy reds; do you have anything new I can try?"

Early in my wine journey, I would get pretty intimidated. I used to stroll into this iconic LA wine shop run by Lou Amdur and gaze at all the cool labels and realize I had no idea what the fuck I was looking at. *Penis D'Aunis? What?* (Turns out it's PINEAU d'Aunis. It's a red wine from the Loire.)

Lou noticed I was lost and grabbed the bottle that I was looking at. He told me about his first experience with the wine—he was on a hiking trip and drank it while roasting lamb and watching shooting stars. He explained how the intense acid in the wine was a result of the vineyard being on a steep slope that caught special gusts of night wind, which is why the fruit is so magical.

Lou didn't care that I didn't know the wine or even the grape variety. A good wine retailer doesn't judge you; they are just excited about wine and excited to share what they know with you. Now when I drink that wine, I have all that cool knowledge that brings me closer to understanding its awesomeness. There may be times when your wine store recommends something you're not into. Be sure to tell them that, and they'll guide you to something else! The low ego level is one of the things I like about the natural wine world. It's chill.

I've been talking a lot about specialty shops because that's really the only place you can find low-intervention wine from smaller, independent wineries and producers. (Most chains and grocery stores don't have a great wine selection; they tend to stock only industrial wine made by big brands at a commodity scale.) If you are serious about buying legit wine, you need to do a little extra work to find a good shop. If you live in Diddlesville, NowhereTown, don't worry, though—a lot of great wine shops will ship to you.

Another option is to buy wine direct from the producer. Many have wine clubs where you can get great discounts and grab rare releases that don't get stocked on shelves.

If you want to take it a step further, buy a plane ticket and visit your favorite producers! If they're more of a lo-fi operation, they probably won't have a tasting room, but you can always just email them and ask if you can visit the winery. I did a lot of this in France, and it's a way to see the real deal. And if you're lucky and very respectful (I've learned just to shut up and not say anything unless asked), they'll cook you some food! It was a super-casual experience and way more fun than a glitzy tasting room. It's freaking beautiful and helps you focus on what you're tasting in an amazing way. It also reinforces the connection between Mother Earth and the bottle in the shop. Some of the most profound experiences of my life have been sipping wine while gazing out over the vines where those exact grapes were grown. Don't forget to take a pic for momma!

ONLINE WINE RETAILERS

Chambers Street Wines:
chambersstwines.com

Discovery Wines: discoverywines.com

Helen's Wines: helenswines.com

Kermit Lynch Wine Merchant:
kermitlynch.com

Kogod Wine Merchant: kogodwine.com

Pairing Wine and Food

Food and wine are best friends. With the proper pairing, both the dish and the sip will be amplified.

I got to experience this concept to its fullest on a trip to the Amalfi Coast of Italy. Madi and I would take a water taxi (which is the coolest thing ever) and pop into these gorgeous seaside restaurants for lunch. They would serve light and bright pastas and amazingly fresh seafood that was fished that morning, like the shrimp linguine on page 126. We'd ask for our server's suggestion of a crisp, local white wine to pair with our dishes, and almost every time they would bring us a salty, minerally Greco. And, oh boy, was it perfection!

A FEW OF MY FAVORITE PAIRINGS

Fried chicken + Champagne

Bo ssäm + Jura reds

Ragù + northern Italian reds

Ceviche + Chenin Blanc

Peking duck + Burgundy

Roast chicken + Beaujolais

Burgers + bubbles (especially a dry pét-nat)

Pizza + Lambrusco

Raw oysters + Chablis

Cheese puffs + Riesling

TIPS FOR THE PERFECT PAIRING

If it grows together, it goes together.
Whenever I travel or cook traditional, regionally specific dishes at home, I always try to drink wine from the same area. In countries such as France and Italy, where the winemaking history goes back centuries, local food specialties evolved alongside the wine. This is why I always drink Burgundy with boeuf bourguignon, and Lambrusco with Emilia-Romagna dishes such as gnocco fritto or prosciutto di Parma.

Sparkling wine is MVP. Whenever I'm feeling stuck and not sure what wine will work with a dish, sparkling wine is the answer. It goes with so many foods. The acid and the bubbles cut through fat and spice in an amazing way, which is why it works well with pizza, anything that's deep-fried, or spicy Thai food. People think of Champagne as a celebration wine, but it's actually one of the most versatile food wines around.

Texture matters more than color. A light-bodied red wine, like Poulsard, is a great pairing for roast chicken. A full-bodied white wine, like an oaky California Chardonnay, will overpower delicate dishes, like raw oysters or steamed fish. So think about the heft and the texture of the wine, not just the color. Pair delicate dishes with lighter, high-acid wines. Heartier food, whether it's a bone-in rib-eye or a chicken with a heavy cream sauce, calls for a heartier, fuller-bodied wine.

Saber Club

When you come over to my house for the first time, you are going to be inducted into a very special club: the Saber Club. My feeling is, why open a bottle of Champagne the boring way? This isn't your graduation dinner at Applebee's!

Sabering, *sabrage* in French, is the tradition of opening sparkling wine with a sword—except it doesn't have to be a sword. The first person I ever saw do it was my friend and co-winemaker, Joel; he used a butter knife to pop open a bottle of his pét-nat. I immediately knew I had to try it. At first, my weapon of choice was the blunt edge of a chef's knife. I'd use that to saber wine at basically *any* event: backyard barbecue, yacht party, children's birthday. I was the saber man.

John C. Reilly saw me do it with my chef's knife often enough that he decided it was time for me to up my saber game. So, he bought me my first sword—a sleek, very modern-looking blade. But I wanted more of a statement saber, so I bought a new saber with a giant gold tassel and a curved steel blade.

No matter what, you have to be careful, because sabering is dangerous! I've had friends slice their hands with the saber, absentmindedly slash themselves on the cut glass of the bottle, and worse. A few macho friends tried to chop the top off the bottle using brute force, which causes the bottle to explode while you're holding it and glass shards to go flying. I used to keep a Breathalyzer on hand at parties, in case some noob tried to saber (or jump off my roof) when too tanked. I like to party, but I don't want my friends ending up in the hospital before the burgies are grilled! So, before you do this at home, promise me a few things: (1) That you'll always start with really cold wine—much colder than cellar temperature. (2) That you'll never, EVER, *EVER* take a swig straight from the bottle—you're going to cut your face open. (3) That you won't put the sabered bottle back in a cooler or ice bucket or fridge—somebody's going to reach in and cut themselves, so just leave it out on the table.

Now that you've been warned, you're allowed to have a li'l saber fun! Here's how to do it, step by step.

Heimy's Sabering How-To

1. Pick out which wine you want to saber. It has to be sparkling—it's the pent-up energy and pressure inside the bottle that makes the whole thing work. In the world of sparkling wines, you have some wines with lots of carbonation and fine bubbles, like Champagne, and some that are very lightly bubbled and low-pressure, like pét-nats. So, ask your wine clerk for something with a lot of carbonation. Keep in mind that you might lose a half-glass of wine due to overflow, so, unless you are Richie Rich, don't saber a crazy-expensive bottle. The bottle itself has to have a lip, so look for bottles that either have a beer-style crown cap or the traditional champagne cork and cage.

2. Chill your wine down so it's *really* cold. That means leave it in the fridge for several hours or in an ice bath for at least 25 minutes. If you're using an ice bath, make sure to chill the bottle upside down for a bit, so the neck gets cold. (When you see a "saber fail"—that is, the neck never breaks or the bottle totally shatters—most of the time it's because the bottle is too warm.)

3. Choose your sabering location. This is key, because when you pop that top, it's going to go flying. It is a deadly weapon! So, fire into the woods, away from your guests/pets/fine art.

4. Choose your sabering music. Something to get you amped up and ready to pound some sparkling wine. I prefer Metallica or the *Game of Thrones* soundtrack.

5. Lift your saber to the heavens and pray to the saber gods for good luck. Present the bottle and saber to the crowd. Ask your guests to touch the bottle and chant, "Respect the saber! Honor the saber!"

6. If the bottle has a cage over the cork, remove the cage. Hold the bottle with your non-dominant hand. If the bottle has a punt (the indented dimple on the bottom of the bottle), stick your thumb in there and cradle the bottle on top of your other four fingers.

7. Every wine bottle has a seam, a thin ridge running the length of the bottle. Find the seam of the bottle and make sure it is facing up. This is your runway.

8. Finally, saber time! Keep in mind that sabering is not about force, it's about finesse, and you can literally do it with a butter knife. Rest your saber at the top of the label, on the seam, at a 45-degree angle. With one confident motion (maintaining contact between sword and wine), run the saber up the neck along the seam toward the cork. When it connects with the lip, the top should fly off and wine will start spraying.

9. Turn the bottle upright and scream a war cry. How loud and long your war cry will depend on where you are in your evening and how many bottles deep you are. Your guests should repeat the war cry and bow. Pour the wine into everyone's glasses, starting with the person with the loudest cry and deepest, most respectful bow. Make sure everyone gets a taste!

Heimy's Most-Sabered Wines

Skip the André and saber something special—you're worth it!

EVERYDAY SABERS

Domaine Brazilier Méthode Trad Brut Rosé: Entry-level saber wine.

Domaine Tissot Crémant du Jura: Stéphane Tissot is one of the best winemakers in the Jura, and his crémant costs half as much as comparable Champagnes.

Jo Landron Atmosphères: Another sparkler from the Loire Valley. Jo Landron has the best mustache of any winemaker, ever. Look it up.

Les Capriades Piège à Filles Rosé: I love this wine's beautiful coral color. It has a bit of sweetness and works really well with spicy food.

Lise et Bertrand Jousset Éxilé: A rosé pét-nat from the Loire Valley.

SPECIAL OCCASION SABERS

Domaine de l'Octavin Betty Bulles: Another great Jura wine; this one is made in pretty small quantities, so if you see a bottle snag it.

Las Jaras Sparkling Old Vines Carignan: Joel's and my sparkling wine, made in the méthode traditionnelle from single-vineyard Carignan with no dosage. Tight bubbles and a nice mousse, perfect for sabering.

St. Reginald Parish Sparkle Motion: A wonderful American wine, made in the Champagne style with 100 percent Oregon Pinot Noir.

EXTREME HAPPY TIMES, MOST-SPECIAL-OCCASION SABERS

Cruse Wine Co. Ultramarine: This is made by my friend, California winemaker Michael Cruse. It's pretty hard to find these days—it's what they call a "cult wine"— so if you track down a bottle, save it for a special sabering occasion.

Jacques Selosse Substance: This is basically the most special Champagne imaginable, made by the father of the natural wine movement in Champagne, Ansleme Selosse. So if you're sabering this beauty, make sure you're sober before you start swinging the sword.

SOME NON-SWORD SABERING TOOLS: A WINE GLASS
(EXPERTS ONLY!), AN IPHONE, A BUTTER KNIFE

Pour Man: The Art of the Porrón

I've always been into exotic drinking devices. This probably dates back to when I was a youth and first encountered the BeerBall. You might think that now that I make and drink a lot of wine, this has gone away. You'd be wrong. If anything, I've become *more* obsessed with drinking devices—they've just become more sophisticated.

Recently, some friends and I constructed a beautiful underwater beer bong, from materials we bought at the hardware store. It's basically a funnel with an on/off plumbing valve, then a tube with ten attachments. After poker nights, we put on some '90s rock—Alice in Chains is good for this—then get in the pool and bong some nice beers. It brings me back to my college days. Sometimes, though, the underwater beer bong doesn't feel quite right. There are moments that call for a slightly more elevated bonging experience.

This is when I break out the porrón.

The porrón is a traditional Spanish wine pitcher that sort of looks like a glass watering can. I love it because it is a device specifically designed for communal drinking. In Spain, you pass it around, and everyone takes a drink by tilting their head backward and tipping the pitcher so that a thin stream of wine shoots out from the spout. The goal is to catch the wine in your mouth without letting your lips touch the spout—after all, everyone's using the same porrón! You get bonus points for extending your pouring arm as far as possible. The longer the stream, the better and more dramatic the porrón.

Fave Wines to Porrón

Why not honor the porrón's country of origin with some nice Spanish wines? Start with white wine to get some practice. Pros in Spain will do it with red wine without getting a spot on their shirts. I'm not there yet.

- **Txakolina:** Pronounced "chock-oh-LEE-nah." A slightly effervescent, super-refreshing white wine from Basque Country. I like producers Bengoetxe and Ameztoi (who also does a rosé).

- **Anything made by Envinate:** One of my fave newish producers; they make wines from the Spanish mainland and the Canary Islands. I've never had a wine from them that I didn't like.

- **Rioja from López de Heredia:** These guys are one of my favorite classic producers, and OGs when it comes to natural winemaking (they were doing indigenous yeasts and no filtration before it was cool). Their Tempranillo-based red wines are most common, but don't sleep on their rich and utterly unique Viura-based white wines.

- **Bichi Pét-Mex:** This isn't from Spain but rather from Mexico. Bichi is a natural producer in Baja, making some of the most exciting wines in that country, perfect for porrón acción.

Spritz Life

Italians have this amazing tradition called the *aperitivo*, and in my ongoing quest to try to be more Italian, I have adopted it into my daily life. Every day, between 4 and 5 p.m., work kind of comes gently to a halt and people wander over to the café to enjoy a cocktail. Visit any Italian town or village, especially in summer, and just watch as people spontaneously gather at the piazza and either sit or stand outside to enjoy a drink.

American happy hours are too aggressive. It's like the work whistle blows, then everyone races to the nearest bar to pound too many beers or cocktails or glasses of wine. In Italy, things are slower and more civilized. The aperitivo hour is a time to collect your thoughts, relax, catch up with friends, and whet your appetite before dinner.

Most bars or restaurants will have snacks on offer. In traditional places, the snacks are set out on platters at the end of the bar and are totally free. If you are a snack freak like me, this is HEAVEN: bars packed with porchetta, salumi, anchovies, the most beautiful olives you've ever seen, breads, and crackers. Grab a little plate of snackies, order a drink, and find a table outside or just sit on the edge of a fountain.

I love to aperitivo, even when I'm home in Los Angeles. Really, you can do it anywhere. But you must follow the aperitivo golden rule, wherever you are: Drink low-ABV! Say no to super-boozy beers and cocktails. Say yes to light, crisp pilsners or cold Prosecco. Or, to be truly dankadent, make yourself a spritz.

A spritz is the simplest and most satisfying cocktail. It's a bit bitter, which gets your stomach rumbling and ready to eat. It's low-alcohol, which is perfect for prolonged partying. And it's always bubbly, through some combination of sparkling wine and seltzer.

To make a spritz, start with an Italian bittersweet liqueur—Aperol is common but a bit sweet for my tastes, so I prefer Campari. Add an equal part of sparkling wine. Top with a splash of soda water, garnish with an olive or an orange slice (or both), and allora! You're spritzed up and ready to go.

Play around with the spritz template, if you'd like, subbing various vermouths, amari, or other aperitivo liqueurs for the Campari. Try a different sparkling wine, like Lambrusco or pét-nat, instead of the Prosecco. It's your spritz life, so live it the way you want.

CAMPARI SPRITZ
WITH AN EXTRA SPLISH

MAKES 1 SERVING

This is my go-to aperitivo order whenever I'm in Italy. It's the perfect move if you're at some random bar or café that doesn't have a great wine program. (Unless you're somewhere that takes its wine really seriously, most Prosecco offered by the glass is mass-produced, too sweet, and kind of bad. The same is true in the United States.) But a Campari Spritz (pictured at right on page 257) is always delicious, even with subpar Prosecco; the bitterness of the Campari cuts through the sweetness of the wine. I always ask for an extra splash of soda water and an extra orange slice.

2 ounces Campari

2 ounces Prosecco

1 ounce club soda, plus more for topping

2 orange slices

Fill a rocks or wine glass with ice, then add the Campari, Prosecco, and club soda and stir gently. Add an extra splash of club soda to the top, for that extra-special bubble experience. Garnish with the orange slices and serve.

AMARO SPRITZ

MAKES 1 SERVING

Amari (see page 262) are a style of Italian after-dinner liqueur. In Italy, it is traditional to drink amari neat; they are super-bitter and are said to help with digestion. Sometimes I'm craving that bitter flavor but don't really want the gut-punch of straight-up amaro. This spritz (pictured at left on page 257) is the answer. Play around with different amari. Averna is on the sweeter side and a good entry-level amaro. Santa Maria al Monte is one of my favorites, but it's very bracing and intense.

2 ounces amaro

3 ounces Prosecco

1 ounce soda water

Orange peel for garnish

Fill a rocks glass with ice, then add the amaro, Prosecco, and soda water and stir. Garnish with the orange peel and serve.

SPRITZ
LIFE

VERMOUTH SPRITZ

MAKES 1 SERVING

2 ounces artisanal rosso/
rouge-style vermouth

4 ounces club soda

Orange slice for garnish

Olive for garnish

I always have a couple bottles of vermouth on hand—white dry vermouth for my martinis, and a red sweet vermouth for Negronis. Until very recently, I always thought about vermouth as a modifier—a backup singer in a cocktail, rather than the star. But recently I've been exploring more artisanal and experimental vermouths; for example, Mauro Vergano's Chinato Americano, which he makes from a base of local Grignolino wine, then infuses with various herbs and aromatics. It kind of lands somewhere between a vermouth and an amaro. The key, I think, is that he starts with high-quality wine, rather than the plonk wine many mainstream vermouth producers use. This recipe is an excuse to go to your local wine or craft spirits shop and ask them if they stock any interesting, artisanal vermouths. In Italy, some winemakers even make a vermouth on the side—it's definitely worth seeking out those bottles.

Fill a rocks or wine glass with ice, then add the vermouth and club soda and stir. Skewer the orange slice and olive on a cocktail pick, garnish, and serve.

NEGRONI SBAGLIATO

MAKES 1 SERVING

1 ounce Campari

1 ounce sweet vermouth

1 ounce Prosecco

Orange slice for garnish

The Negroni (page 268) is one of my all-time favorite drinks but, since it's gin-based, it's sometimes a bit strong for aperitivo hour. The Negroni Sbagliato (pictured at center, opposite) is a lower-ABV version that subs Prosecco for gin. *Sbagliato* is Italian for "mistaken" or "incorrect"—so, basically, this is a Negroni that somebody, somewhere, messed up. We're glad they did because this drink is perfect.

This is a great one to scale up for a party. Just combine equal parts Prosecco, Campari, and vermouth in a punch bowl filled with giant ice cubes and float orange slices on the top.

Fill a rocks or wine glass with ice, then add the Campari, vermouth, and Prosecco and stir. Garnish with the orange slice and serve.

COCKTAILS

My home bar has one spirit only: FIREBALL.

I love cinnamon so much I was overjoyed when I learned I could have it in alcoholic form.

NOOOOOO!!!OOOO!!O!O!!OOOO!!!OO!!!

Just kidding. With my bar cart, I like to keep things minimal and pick a few really nice bottles that tell a story. To me, that means a spirit made in the traditional or "ancestral" way, from raw materials that are unique to the region in which they are grown.

The Camut brothers make beautiful Calvados on their farm in Normandy, France. They grow apples in their family's orchard. And when the apples fall from the trees, the Camuts turn them into cider. They distill the cider in the pot still that their father built in the 1950s, and age the brandy in barrels, some of which have been in the family since before World War I. You may not think you like apple brandy, but when you taste the Camut brothers' Calvados, you realize that you are drinking history. This is a truly artisanal product created from amazing local produce, transformed by a copper pot and live fire. It could only be made by these guys in this specific place—and in that way, it tells a story.

When I visited Puerto Rico for the first time to shoot a Todd Solondz film, I got really into Barrilito's, a local rum that dates back to the late 1800s. If you grew up drinking Bacardi Silver or Malibu (sadly, we've all been there), then you probably associate rum with nasty sweet drinks and high school hangovers. But rum is one of the most diverse categories of any spirit, and the best rums are complex, funky, and profound. I'd stack a beautiful aged rum up against a luxury whiskey any day. Barrilito's Three-Star is one of those Holy Grail rums for me: It's made in a family-run operation (I've heard that the factory in Bayamón has only nine employees, four of whom are in the family) and aged in Oloroso sherry casks. If you can find it, the three-star bottling will blow your mind. It's a blend of rums aged for six to ten years and has a deep, almondy brown hue. In Puerto Rico, the locals sip it out of plastic cups filled with ice. When I sip it at home—over ice, or occasionally with a bit of sugar and lime, Ti' Punch style—I'm immediately transported back to Puerto Rico and its beautiful, sandy beaches.

I love a gin martini (see page 267), and when done right—with ice made from purified water and beautiful glassware—even a gin and tonic can be an elevated drink. So I've always got to have gin on hand. My favorites are made by California's St. George Spirits, one of the few truly independent distilleries in the United States. Try their Terroir bottling, which uses Douglas fir and California bay laurel as aromatics. It smells like a hike through Northern California, and makes a beautiful martini.

In addition to those, you'll find green Chartreuse, a French herbal liqueur made by Carthusian monks from a secret recipe dating back to the 1700s; some unmarked bottles of mezcal that I brought home from Oaxaca; and a Czech plum brandy called Šljivovica that my friend Lucia sent me. The Heimy Bar is all about those singular spirits that take me on a journey.

Bitter Boys: Amaro 101

In this book, you've learned about the importance of acid and to embrace beige in your cooking. Now here comes yet another life-changing taste lesson: BRING ON THE BITTER.

I'm sure you've seen those nuclear-red bottles of Campari at even the diviest bars. And if you've enjoyed the bittersweet flavor, then you might be ready to graduate to amari (the plural of amaro). Whereas Campari and Aperol are considered aperitivi—they're meant to be consumed before a meal—amari are traditionally considered digestivi—postmeal sippers.

There's an art to mastering the long, gorgeous, memorable meal. You start with a Vermouth Spritz (page 256) or some other well-made cocktail to get your taste buds charged up. You drink your wines in a progression from lightest to heaviest. Then at the end, you sip a tummy-tingling amaro. It's your medicine (that also tastes amazing and keeps your buzz alive). The flavor of amaro is incredibly bracing, herbaceous, and bitter. It's the liquid equivalent of smelling salts. (But in a beautiful way.) It settles your stomach and perks you back up.

Amaro's ancestral home is in Italy—in fact, the word *amaro* is Italian for "bitter." Amari are made by macerating (and in some cases, distilling) botanicals such as bark, seeds, herbs, flowers, and spices in a base spirit or wine and then sweetening it.

If you travel in Italy, you'll discover that many towns and regions have their own signature amaro. In Valtellina, up in the mountains of Lombardy near the border with Switzerland, you'll find Bràulio, an amazingly herbal amaro that smells like an Alpine hillside. In the seaside town of Genoa, there's Santa Maria al Monte, one of my favorites, which tastes like a delicious mix of spearmint and cola. In Milan, find a café by the Piazza del Duomo and order Zucca Rabarbaro, an elegant amaro with notes of rhubarb. I could go on—there are hundreds of amari out there, and many of them are not yet imported to the States.

You don't have to buy a plane ticket to go on a little amaro journey. In the past few years, in-the-know bars and restaurants in the United States have really embraced amari. They've become a bit of a trade secret among industry types. Ordering an amaro is like a Bat Signal informing your bartender that you know what's up. (That's why ordering a shot of Fernet-Branca is called "the bartender's handshake.")

The bar at Osteria Mozza in Los Angeles has an incredible selection and if you're extra nice to the bartender, and don't tell them I told you, they MIGHT just let you try some of their special stash. In NYC, Amor y Amargo is my spot for a post-dinner amaro. Just don't tell anyone about it. Okay?

AMARI TO TRY

I'm a devoted Bitter Boy, and I want to make you an amaro convert too. Here, I list a few of my favorites. I've ranked them from least to most assertive and intense. So, if you're new to intensely bitter flavors, start at the top of the list and work your way down. I drink mine with one ice cube and an orange peel for garnish.

- Amaro Averna—Caltanissetta, Sicily
- Amaro dell'Erborista—Muccia, Marche
- Amaro Nardini—Bassano del Grappa, Veneto
- Amaro Sibilla—Muccia, Marche
- Santa Maria al Monte—Genoa, Liguria; this is the nectar of the gods!
- Zucca Rabarbaro—Milan, Lombardy

Cocktails You Should Memorize by Heart

My cocktail philosophy is that simple is best. I like drinks that are alcohol forward, made with good ingredients and technique. That means no twelve-component drinks, no bad ice, no glassware that is still warm from the dishwasher. Take the time to chill your glasses before serving. Stir your drinks properly—this isn't just to chill them, it's also to dilute them. (Water is an important ingredient in cocktails.) Invest in nice all-purpose coupe glasses, Collins glasses, and old-fashioned glasses.

The eight recipes that follow are the classics that every drinker should know how to make. Cheers!

MANHATTAN

MAKES 1 SERVING

Transport yourself to a dark, classy bar in New York City with this perfect cocktail. Most of the time, I drink my whiskey neat or over one large ice cube. I respect the liquor! When I'm feeling sassy, I'll go for a Manhattan.

In a mixing glass filled with ice, combine the bourbon, vermouth, and both bitters. Stir until chilled, then strain into a martini or coupe glass. Garnish with the cherry and serve.

2 ounces bourbon or rye

1 ounce sweet vermouth

2 dashes Angostura bitters

1 dash orange bitters

Brandied cherry for garnish

MARGARITA

MAKES 1 SERVING

Moving to Los Angeles during the middle of the Mixology Boom had its perks. Tasting a REAL margarita without the bullshit of premade, synthetic mixers was game changing. While the traditional recipe for a margarita calls for tequila and an orange liqueur, like Cointreau or Triple Sec, I love a mezcal margarita. It's a touch smokier and more complex than tequila versions. Too smoky for ya? Split the base: 1 ounce mezcal, 1 ounce tequila.

In a shaker filled with ice, combine the mezcal, lime juice, and agave syrup. Shake until chilled, then strain into a rocks glass filled with fresh ice. Garnish with the lime wedge and serve.

2 ounces mezcal

1 ounce lime juice

¾ ounce agave syrup (1 part agave nectar dissolved in 1 part water)

Lime wedge for garnish

DAIQUIRI

MAKES 1 SERVING

This has nothing to do with the crazy-sweet, blended "fruit" daiquiris you get on the beach. I'm talking about the elegant, classic cocktail that Hemingway used to drink in Cuba in the 1940s. Try to find a nice white rum for this—I like Diplomático.

In a shaker filled with ice, combine the rum, lime juice, and simple syrup. Shake until chilled, then strain into a coupe glass. Garnish with the lime wheel and serve.

2 ounces white rum

¾ ounce lime juice

¾ ounce simple syrup (1 part sugar dissolved in 1 part water)

Lime wheel for garnish

MARTINI

MAKES 1 SERVING

I'm a gin martini guy. Plain and simple. One of my favorite rituals is sinking into a big squishy leather chair at the bar of a dimly lit steakhouse while sipping an ice-cold martini. I order either a dry gin martini with an olive (I can't resist house-made blue cheese–stuffed olives) or a Gibson, a martini variation with a pickled onion and onion brine. I sit back and watch quietly as the maestro goes to work. He stirs the ingredients until they're icy cold, then fills up the tiny V-shaped glass until it's on the brink of overflowing. He slides the glass to me with a smile, and it's up to me to carefully raise it to my lips so as not to spill a drop. Recently I experienced the martini trolley at the Connaught Bar in London—a bartender wheels it up to you, you select the gin, vermouth, and bitters you'd like to use, and he stirs up the drink right at your tableside. It's a beautiful art form to watch; each step is painstakingly perfect and makes you enjoy each sip even more.

I'm very particular about my martini. First, the gin has to be amazing. For a drink that is pretty much all gin, this is a no-brainer. I love to use St. George Spirits Terroir bottling with its beautiful herbaceous essence.

Next, I like a dry martini. (*Dry* refers to the amount of vermouth in the drink.) I pour a tiny measure in the glass, swish it around, and dump it out. Just a whisper of vermouth.

Temperature is essential. Ten minutes before I'm ready to make my 'tini, I put my glass, mixing glass, jigger, AND barspoon in the freezer.

My final particularity is dilution. I need it be stirred just so, to allow the ice to melt and integrate to create the perfect martini.

If all of this sounds like a lot of work, good. Respect the craft. It should take time to make a perfect drink. The martini is my favorite cocktail of all time because it's a drink steeped in ritual.

Dry vermouth for rinsing

2¼ ounces gin

Castelvetrano or blue cheese–stuffed olives for garnish

Pour a splash of vermouth into a martini or Nick and Nora glass, swirl to coat the glass, and then discard any excess. Place the gin in a mixing glass filled with ice and stir until chilled and diluted. Strain into the prepared glass, garnish with the olives, and serve.

Note: To make a mini-tini, just split the recipe among two smaller glasses. A lot of the time, a mini-tini is all you really need.

NEGRONI

MAKES 1 SERVING

Orange peel for garnish, plus
1 orange slice (optional)

1 ounce gin

1 ounce Campari

1 ounce sweet vermouth

My first cocktail love was the Negroni. It's big and bold but has a lot of class. Maybe it's because it's from Italy, and I love everything Italian. But I really just think it's a perfect cocktail, with a balance of sweet, bitter, and boozy. It also helps that it's the easiest possible recipe to remember: 1-1-1.

Rub the orange peel around the edge of a rocks glass, for the ultimate aromatic experience, and add one large ice cube. In a mixing glass filled with ice, combine the gin, Campari, and vermouth; and if you're in a juicy mood, squeeze in a bit of orange juice from the orange slice. Stir until chilled, then strain into the prepared glass. Garnish with the orange peel and serve.

CORPSE REVIVER NO. 2

MAKES 1 SERVING

Joel Burt introduced me to this cocktail on one of our many sales trips. This is the drink for when you've had one too many glasses of wine the night before. It's fresh and citrusy, with just a hint of bracing bitterness from the absinthe. It'll revive you. This is what industry people call an "equal-parts drink": there's 1 ounce of every ingredient, so it's an easy recipe to remember, even when you're feeling a bit foggy.

Absinthe for rinsing

1 ounce gin

1 ounce Cointreau

1 ounce Lillet

1 ounce lemon juice

Lemon or orange twist for garnish

Pour a splash of absinthe into a coupe glass, swirl to coat the glass, and then discard any excess. In a shaker filled with ice, combine the gin, Cointreau, Lillet, and lemon juice. Shake until chilled, then strain into the prepared glass. Garnish with the citrus twist and serve.

HIGHBALL

MAKES 1 SERVING

2 ounces spirit of choice

Club soda for topping

Lemon peel for squeezing
(optional)

This hardly counts as a recipe. A highball is basically just whisky plus club soda over ice. But a well-made highball is a beautiful thing. I got turned on to highballs when I was in Japan; as with most things, they've truly mastered the art there. In fact, Japanese whisky company Suntory has even developed a highball machine. It chills the whisky and water to the proper temperature; then, when the bartender pulls a tap (it almost looks like they're pulling a draft beer), the machine dispenses a perfectly carbonated whisky-soda mixture. They've also made highball cans that are available at any convenience store. It's the best.

The nice thing about a highball is that you get to experience the flavors of the pure spirit, but you also stay hydrated! So it's perfect for those times when you want to appreciate a spirit neat . . . but don't want to get wasted.

Last, but most important of all: Use good ice for this. Don't use ice that's been sitting in your freezer for six months and has absorbed all your nasty freezer smells. Don't use cheap party ice from the bodega, because it will melt in five seconds and dilute your drink too much. DO buy 1-inch ice molds and make the ice from purified water. This is such a simple drink, so every little detail matters.

Fill a highball glass with ice, then pour in the spirit. Top with the club soda, then, if desired, squeeze the essence of the lemon peel over the drink and discard the peel. Serve immediately.

BLOODY MARY

MAKES 1 SERVING

Part of the beauty of the martini (see page 267) is its elegance—
it's an exercise in restraint. The beauty of the Bloody Mary is that it's
completely ridiculous and extravagant. I embrace them both. I'm a
man of contrasts.

Do you need to include all of the garnishes listed here in your Bloody
Mary? No, of course not. But this is one of the rare instances where I'm
encouraging you to be totally extreme. Get a bit artsy with your garnishes.
Try to cut your pickles, carrots, and radishes so they're roughly the same
size, to make them aesthetically pleasing. Get a bunch of toothpicks or
cocktail picks and make several attractive skewers; maybe fold a paper-
thin slice of lemon and skewer that, then weave a whole anchovy on the
same pick, followed by another folded slice of lemon. On another pick,
alternate between olives and slices of cured meat. Be creative.

Be warned: My signature Pepper in My Bepper Bloody Mary Mix has a bit
of a kick to it. Typically, if I'm reaching for a Bloody Mary, it means I'm
a little bit hungover, so you know I'm gonna need that spice to perk me
back up.

1 In a pint glass filled with ice, combine the Bloody Mary mix and vodka
and stir until chilled.

2 To garnish: Arrange any of your garnish choices in the glass. The celery
stalk is the final touch—you need that to stir your drink around as you sip.

3 Serve immediately.

In a large pitcher, combine the tomato juice, lemon juice, Worcestershire,
Sriracha, horseradish, clam juice (if using), celery salt, and kosher salt;
season with pepper; and stir. If not using immediately, store airtight in
the fridge for up to 1 week.

4 ounces Pepper in My
Bepper Bloody Mary
Mix (recipe follows)

2 ounces vodka

Garnishes

Dill pickle spear, halved
or quartered lengthwise

Baby carrots and French
breakfast radishes, quartered
lengthwise

Cured meats (such as
saucisson sec, chorizo,
or sopressata), sliced into
⅛-inch coins

Olives

Anchovies and other
tinned fish

Thinly sliced lemon

Celery stalk with leaves

PEPPER IN MY BEPPER BLOODY MARY MIX

MAKES 4½ CUPS, ENOUGH
FOR 9 SERVINGS

4 cups tomato juice

¼ cup lemon juice

¼ cup Worcestershire sauce

¼ cup Sriracha

5 tablespoons prepared
horseradish

2 tablespoons clam juice
(optional)

2 teaspoons celery salt

1 teaspoon kosher salt

Freshly ground black pepper

BLISS MODE PARTY

Let's go full bliss mode now! We are all gonna drift off to the big sleep one day. But until then, embrace life! Grab your closest BFFs, sculpt an ice luge, eat some caviar, and celebrate today. Reflect on all the reasons why food and wine are so beautiful and enriching, but have a sense of humor about it. That's the Heimy Way. Chef's Kiss to you all!

CAVIAR LIFESTYLE

The best way to enjoy caviar is on a humble potato chip. Buy regular, unflavored chips—not too salty because you don't want to overpower the delicate caviar flavor. Chef José Andrés's brand works well for this. Maybe a tiny spoonful of crème fraîche. Then a tiny spoonful of caviar.

If you don't want to break the bank on caviar, keep an eye out for ikura, which is Japanese cured salmon roe. It's a totally different experience than caviar—the roe is much bigger and pops with a more assertive briny flavor. But ikura is still fish eggs and it's still delicious.

HOW TO SHUCK OYSTERS

You're going to need to buy an oyster shucker and glove. Don't be crazy and shuck bare-handed—even pros use gloves to ensure that (a) they have a good grip on the oyster and the slippery guy doesn't fly away, (b) they don't stab themselves with the knife, and (c) they don't cut themselves on a jagged edge of a shell (this is actually the most common oyster-related injury).

1. Place the glove on your non-dominant hand.

2. Place the oyster on a clean work surface with the hinge facing toward you and hold it down firmly with your gloved hand. (If you're a real pro, you can firmly cup the oyster in the palm of your gloved hand.)

3. Slip the tip of the oyster knife into the hinge of the oyster (the blade should be parallel to the seam of the oyster). Give the knife a good little wiggle and push to ensure it's stuck in there firmly and that you have leverage.

4. Once the tip of the oyster knife is securely stuck in the hinge, turn the knife 90 degrees so that its blade is now perpendicular to the oyster's seam. The hinge should pop open.

5. Wiggle your knife in again and run it around the top shell to release it. Discard the top shell.

6. Now run your knife under the oyster to release the muscle from the shell. Be careful to spill as little of that sweet, sweet oyster juice as possible!

7. Place the bottom oyster shell with the now-released oyster muscle on a bed of ice and continue with the remaining oysters.

Simple Mignonette

In a small serving bowl, combine ¼ cup red wine vinegar, 1 tablespoon minced shallots, and a few healthy cranks of fresh black pepper. Bonus points for finding a tiny spoon to serve it with. (I love tiny spoons.)

HOW TO MAKE A SHRIMP COCKTAIL

It's up to you on how extreme you want to go with this. You could just intersperse the shrimp on the same bed of ice as your oysters. You could also put the cocktail sauce in a martini glass and ring the shrimp around the edge. *Or* you could take your cue from Salvador Dalí, who threw epic, beautifully surreal dinner parties, and build a giant shrimp tower. Guess which one I'm gonna do?

1. Buy nice, big shell-on shrimp.

2. Fill a large pot with water and season with 1 tablespoon Old Bay Seasoning. Prepare an ice bath.

3. Set the pot over medium-high heat. You are NOT looking for a boil here; you are looking for a temperature that I like to call "ow hot." Basically it's the temperature where the water is too hot for you to keep your finger in it for a long time. For those of you not looking to scald your fingers, pull out your thermometer and let it reach 150°F.

4. Once the water is at the right temperature, add the shrimp and cook just until they are pink and beginning to curl. It shouldn't take longer than 3 minutes. If you overcook them, they'll be rubbery.

5. Immediately drain the shrimp and transfer to the ice bath. Shell them and present them as beautifully and creatively as you can! A martini glass works well here as the vessel.

Extra Horseradish-y Cocktail Sauce

In a small serving bowl, combine ½ cup ketchup, three big spoonfuls of horseradish, a spoonful of lemon juice, and several shakes of Worcestershire and hot sauce and stir to incorporate. Dip away!

WINE PAIRINGS

Serving shrimp and white wine together is actually a super-legit pairing. (But drink the good stuff, obviously.) Crisp, high-acid wines work great with seafood, especially white wines with saline notes (Muscadet) or pronounced minerality (Chablis, dry styles of Chenin Blanc, Assyrtiko). These are some of my favorite bottles.

- Anjou Blanc from Thibaud Boudignon (region: Loire Valley; grape: Chenin Blanc)

- Chablis from Domaine Moreau-Naudet (region: northern Burgundy; grape: Chardonnay)

- Las Jaras "Waves" in a can (region: California; grape: French Colombard)

- Muscadet from Domaine de la Pépière (region: Loire Valley; grape: Melon de Bourgogne)

BLISS MODE
ACHIEVED

Acknowledgments

Thank you to Mom and Dad for always supporting and encouraging me, even though my ideas and interests were always a li'l "wild."

Thank you to Madi for being my personal food and wine taster, travel partner, and cat wrangler. You build me up to be the best I can be.

Thank you to my incredible coauthor and partner in *Foodheim*, Emily Timberlake, a person I don't have to explain the concept of Circle Foods to! She and her now-husband's first date was at a Tim & Eric live show. We were destined to make this thing together.

I am so grateful to all the food and wine gurus who guided me on my culinary journey. Special thanks to chefs Grant Achatz, Erik Anderson, Joe Beddia, Dave Beran, Chris Bianco, Thomas Borbely, Danny Bowein, Sean Brock, Noel Brohner, Michael Carlson, Joseph Centeno, David Chang, Michael Cimarusti, Chad Colby, Vinny Dotolo, Aaron Franklin, Evan Funke, Kevin Gillespie, Jon Gray, Ilan Hall, Brooks Headley, Eric Kim, Chris Kronner, Matty Matheson, Ori Menashe, René Redzepi, Chad Robertson, Ben Shewry, Jon Shook, Nancy Silverton, Jeremiah Stone, Craig Thornton, Kat Turner, Daniele Uditi, Marc Vetri, Fabián von Hauske, and Kris Yenbamroong for their friendship and all the tasty bites. To Lou Amdur, Amy Atwood, Mike Bennie, Jill Bernheimer, Patrick Cappiello, Robert Dentice, Vinny Eng, Camille Fourmont, Helen Johannsen, Trevor Kellog, Andrew Mariani, Rajat Parr, J.D. Plotnick, Marissa Ross, the staff at Silverlake Wines, and Devon Tarby, thank you for sharing your expertise and so many beautiful wines and spirits over the years.

Thank you to Josh Modell for being my Chicago wingman, and to Chloe Wise and Carly Mark for thousands of Troy dinners. Thanks to Alexis Florio and Will Forte for introducing me to good LA sushi, and to Tim Heidecker for putting up with all the insane Japanese business meals I would set up. (And for letting me make you try sea cucumber.) Thanks to John C. Reilly for taking me around Sicily and mainland Italy and introducing me to Chef's Life.

I could never have become the wine freak I am today without my great friend and partner and dough consultant at Las Jaras, Joel Burt. Thank you for making my winemaking dreams a reality. Thanks also to all our farming partners in California and Oregon. Grazie mille to everyone who welcomed me so warmly to Italy and taught me about the food traditions of your amazing country, especially Katie Parla and chef Massimo Bottura. To my fellow Food Club Captains Aziz Ansari, Alan Yang, and Jason Woliner, and skippers Jon Shook and Vinny Dotolo. You opened up the doors on my culinary journey. Thank you to Cream Co. Meats and Ian Purkayastha of Regalis Foods for all the sweet meat and sea treats, and to Made In for supplying me with cook gear. Thanks to Ellen Bennett, Sue Chan, Jonathan Gold, Ollie Green, Daniel Greenberg, James Murphy, Karen O, Questlove, and T-Pain for everything you do. Thanks to Mike

Rosen for making the pitch deck that practically sold this book by itself. STOLDS, GGP, Ladies Night, you know who you are and what you mean to me. Duke Aber, you are my design prince and I bow to you. Thank you to the wonderful publishing team at Ten Speed Press, including Erica Gelbard, Mari Gill, Doug Ogan, Serena Sigona, and Daniel Wikey. Special shout-out to art director Emma Campion and editor Kelly Snowden for being the best collaborators. I am in awe of our talented photographer and photography team. Thank you to Julia Stotz, Caroline Hwang, Samantha Margherita, Yasara Gunawardena, and Jessica Darakjian for always going the extra mile and working so hard to create something so dang beautiful. And for also not letting me call a recipe "Flesh Tower."

—Eric Wareheim

Biggest thanks, of course, go to Eric Wareheim for being the most generous and fun collaborator a gal could ask for. Thank you for being such a dream to work with, teaching me so much, and letting me throw an ice sculpture of your head into the hot tub. We couldn't have done this project without Madison Borbely, an outrageously talented cook, recipe writer, garganelli maker, rib model . . . the list goes on. To my Ten Speed Press queens Kelly Snowden and Emma Campion: Thank you for blessing this project with your many talents, believing in us, always steering us in the right direction, skimming the pool, and being the best damned publishing team in the biz. Thank you to David Black and Rica Allanic at the David Black Agency for their support and sage counsel. Thank you to Duke Aber for being brilliant and always game. To our impossibly talented and fun-to-be-around photo team: Julia Stotz, Caroline Hwang, Samantha Margherita, Yasara Gunawardena, and Jessica Darakjian, you all are truly the best and we were so lucky to work with you. Many rounds on me next time! To my pals and ever-willing food testers Daniel Rojas, Matt Cagle, Steph Hall, Peter Richmond, Ellen Richmond, Pete Smith, and Annie Chabel, thank you for always being down to eat pasta and pizza and burgies. To Rebecca Elliott and Jessie Katz: Shame on you for living too far away for me to cook for you (I love you anyways). To Kaitlin Ketchum, thank you for being an amazing friend, confidant, advisor, and indulger in batshit-crazy fan theories. Thank you to my brother, Teddy, for being a man I could be a best friend with; to my mom, MaryGael, for being the best cook (and mom) I know; and to my dad, Ted, who has probably already bought ten copies and launched a grassroots marketing campaign. But most of all, thank you to Ethan Forrest, without whom I would be a sad, cat-less bag of bones. I love you.

—Emily Timberlake

About the Authors

Eric Wareheim is a director, actor, writer, comedian, and winemaker. He is half of comedy duo Tim & Eric, who have been making TV shows, movies, books, and music for twenty years. Wareheim also directed, produced, and starred in Netflix series *Master of None*. He runs the world's Top Food Blog and has a cinnamon-colored cat named Gino.

Emily Timberlake writes about food, wine, and pop culture and is a former senior editor at Ten Speed Press. She lives in Oakland, California.

Index

Published in the United States by Ten Speed Press, an
imprint of Random House, a division of Penguin Random
House LLC, New York.
www.tenspeed.com

Ten Speed Press and the Ten Speed Press colophon are
registered trademarks of Penguin Random House LLC.

Library of Congress Control Number: 2021936800

Library of Congress Cataloging-in-Publication Data
is on file with the publisher.

Hardcover ISBN: 978-1-9848-5852-8
eBook ISBN: 978-1-9848-5853-5

Printed in China

Editor: Kelly Snowden | Production editor: Doug Ogan |
Art Director/designer: Emma Campion | Cover designer:
Duke Aber | Production designer: Mari Gill | Production
manager: Serena Sigona | Prepress color manager: Jane
Chinn | Wardrobe stylist: Beverly Nguyen | Food stylist:
Caroline K. Hwang | Food stylist assistant: Jessica Darakjian |
Prop stylist: Samantha Margherita | Prop sytlist assistant:
Jennelle Fung | Photo assistant: Yasara Gunawardena |
Photo re-toucher: Brian Guldo | Recipe developer: Chris
Kronner | Copyeditor: Nancy Bailey | Proofreader: Linda
M. Bouchard | Indexer: Michael Goldstein | Publicist: Erica
Gelbard | Marketer: Daniel Wikey

Page 58: Sculpture by Carly Mark.
Page 211: Painting by Chloe Wise.
Page 233: Drawing by Sarah Rabin.
Page 237: Drawing by Carly Mark.

10 9 8 7 6 5 4 3 2 1

First Edition